ACCLAIM FOR FAYE LEVY AND HER PREVIOUS BOOK,

30 LOW-FAT MEALS IN 30 MINUTES

"Faye Levy's recipes always are inviting, but the bonus here—in addition to being low-fat—is that the dishes and menus are easy."
— *Oregonian*

"Whole meals in half an hour. Now there's a challenge. Levy takes on our two favorite adjectives—fast and low-fat—and makes meals that are both."
— *Newsday*

"Something of value for any cook....The recipes [are] excellent, clearly described, and easily followed."
— *KLIATT*

"Faye Levy ranks among the most imaginative and careful of all cookbook authors."
— *Boston Herald*

"As an instructor and inspiration in the kitchen, Faye Levy is without peer."
— **Maureen Clancy,** *San Diego Union-Tribune*

"Levy is one of our brightest new cookbook authors. As meticulous and painstaking as she is creative, Levy, always the teacher, gives impeccable instructions."
— *Cleveland Plain Dealer*

"Her recipes always work and the information she imparts is always easily understood by every level of cook."
— **Muriel Stevens,** *Las Vegas Sun*

"Levy is one of the most knowledgeable and reliable food writers in the country."
— **Judith Hill, food editor,** *First for Women*

"Levy is one of America's top culinary columni͏ ͏nd authors."
— *Elle*

P9-DEM-873

30 Low-Fat Meals in 30 Minutes

Faye Levy's International Vegetable Cookbook

Faye Levy's International Chicken Cookbook

Faye Levy's International Jewish Cookbook

Sensational Pasta

Sensational Chocolate

Fresh from France: Dessert Sensations

Fresh from France: Dinner Inspirations

Fresh from France: Vegetable Creations

Classic Cooking Techniques

La Cuisine du Poisson (in French, with Fernand Chambrette)

Faye Levy's Favorite Recipes (in Hebrew)

French Cooking Without Meat (in Hebrew)

French Desserts (in Hebrew)

French Cakes, Pastries and Cookies (in Hebrew)

The La Varenne Tour Book

30 LOW-FAT VEGETARIAN MEALS IN 30 MINUTES

Faye Levy

WARNER BOOKS

A Time Warner Company

If you purchase this book without a cover you should be aware that this book may have been stolen property and reported as "unsold and destroyed" to the publisher. In such case neither the author nor the publisher has received any payment for this "stripped book."

Copyright © 1997 by Faye Levy
All rights reserved.

Warner Books, Inc., 1271 Avenue of the Americas, New York, NY 10020
Visit our Web site at
http://pathfinder.com/twep

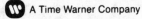 A Time Warner Company

Printed in the United States of America
First Printing: March 1997
10 9 8 7 6 5 4 3 2 1

Library of Congress Cataloging-in-Publication Data

Levy, Faye.
    30 low-fat vegetarian meals in 30 minutes / Faye Levy.
       p. cm.
    Includes index.
    ISBN 0-446-67211-4
    1. Vegetarian cookery. 2. Quick and easy cookery. 3. Low-fat diet—Recipes.
4. Menus. I. Title.
TX837.L468 1997
641.5'636—dc20
                                         96-7225
                                         CIP

Book design and composition by L&G McRee
Cover design by Nancy Silva/Don Puckey

ATTENTION: SCHOOLS AND CORPORATIONS
WARNER books are available at quantity discounts with bulk purchase for educational, business, or sales promotional use. For information, please write to: SPECIAL SALES DEPARTMENT, WARNER BOOKS, 1271 AVENUE OF THE AMERICAS, NEW YORK, N.Y. 10020

CONTENTS

CONTENTS

INTRODUCTION

I have always been tempted by vegetarian menus. Instead of relegating vegetables to secondary ingredients overshadowed by meat, a vegetarian menu elevates them to the leading role. By focusing on meatless dishes, vegetarian cooks around the world have come up with countless delicious creations using greens and grains.

The value of vegetarian cuisine, however, goes far beyond its contribution to gastronomy. To many, the proven health benefits of low-fat vegetarian fare are the best reason for chasing meat from their menus. Vegetarians also emphasize the importance of compassion for animals and point out the benefit to the earth—vegetarian food is much less of a drain on the world's resources than meat-based diets. In the home kitchen, meatless meals are clearly the most economical.

Nutritionists recommend that we eat five or more servings of vegetables and fruits a day as a way to promote good health and resist disease. After all, vegetables and fruits contribute to our diet nearly all the vitamins and minerals we need, yet they contain little or no fat, are low in calories, and have no cholesterol. Following a vegetarian diet practically guarantees that we'll get the desired amounts of vegetables and fruits.

Although we now realize the merits of vegetarian cooking, we still are faced with the time constraints of modern life. Our busy lifestyles don't leave us much time to spend in the kitchen. We want dishes that we can prepare quickly and effortlessly, with ingredients that we can find easily at the supermarket.

I have devoted many months to developing these kinds of recipes: vegetarian, fast to prepare, and low in fat. Most of the menus in this book have short ingredient lists and do not require many pots. When I was working on my previous book, *30 Low-Fat Meals in 30 Minutes*, my challenge was to create quick, easy, wholesome, and lively menus that were low in fat. In this book, I have gone even further: I have designed menus that are low in cholesterol as well and completely meatless. They do *not* require eggs and some have *no* dairy products.

Following the accepted nutritional standards, I have limited the calories from fat in each menu to no more than 30 percent, with minimal saturated fat. In fact, in nearly half of the menus, I have pared down the calories from fat to 20 percent or less, with the lowest at only 9 percent.

Cooking fast, low-fat vegetarian meals is simpler today than ever. There is an impressive number of low-fat and fat-free ingredients in the store, and more are coming all the time. Many new products, from oil-free tortilla chips to nonfat sour cream to fat-free yogurt, actually taste great and give us many leaner choices for our meals. I find them useful additions to quick, low-fat menus. Our markets also provide time-saving ingredients, such as already-washed greens, shredded carrots, and sliced mushrooms. And don't forget: keeping to a low-fat diet is much easier with meatless menus, because vegetarian foods tend to be naturally low in fat.

I hope this book will be an inspiring and useful guide for anyone who wishes to prepare healthful, tasty menus in a flash. Saving time cooking should help us take pleasure in relaxed, leisurely eating, which—who knows?—may be as important for our well-being as good nutrition.

30 Low-Fat Vegetarian Meals in 30 Minutes

CHAPTER 1

STRATEGIES FOR FAST, LOW-FAT VEGETARIAN COOKING

Since vegetarian cooking relies greatly on beans and grains, which tend to have long cooking times, it might seem impossible to prepare meals quickly. Fortunately, there are many ways to get around this obstacle. Knowing how to shop and where to look for time-saving ingredients is essential. When you *do* use long-cooking ingredients, save time by cooking enough for several meals.

Saving time and lowering the fat in your meals begins at the market. Be sure your pantry, refrigerator, and freezer contain the basics for quick, healthful meals for those days when you don't have time to buy fresh ingredients.

To get a meal on the table fast, it's important to cook efficiently. Have a plan of action to make the best use of your time. Try to have several dishes cooking simultaneously. Each of these menus spells out how to do this, and soon you'll find it easy to think up simple timetables for menus of your own.

MENU PLANNING AND SHOPPING

Vegetarian menus are often much more flexible than conventional ones. For example, they don't necessarily include a first course, main course, and dessert. A vegetable stew accompanied by rice and a salad can make a satisfying, easy dinner. Soup and a sandwich are an American supper favorite, and they work very well in vegetarian form, too.

Some think vegetarian food is complicated and is full of cheese and nuts. However, meatless cooking can be easy and delicious without these high-fat ingredients.

Fortunately, the ingredients necessary for speedy vegetarian cooking are available at the supermarket. A careful look at the items in many different aisles of the market will reveal a surprising number of foods that fit in well with low-fat meatless cooking. There is no need to search for them in health food stores. But if you do visit such stores from time to time, you'll find even more choices.

There is also some concern about how to get enough protein and other nutrients in a vegetarian diet. In fact, planning a balanced menu is easy using the USDA Food Guide Pyramid. A meal will most likely include foods from the Bread, Cereal, Rice & Pasta Group (the base of the pyramid) and probably either a dairy product, dried beans, or occasionally nuts or eggs. Naturally, it will include a variety of fruits and vegetables, whether cooked, raw, or some of each.

Here is a summary of what the USDA Food Guide Pyramid allows per day:

At the base of the pyramid, foods to eat the most:
• 6–11 servings in the Bread, Cereal, Rice & Pasta Group
Examples of 1 serving are: 1 slice of bread; 1 ounce of ready-to-eat cereal; ½ cup of cooked cereal, rice, or pasta; 5–6 small crackers.

Just above the base of the pyramid, foods to eat in generous amounts:
• 3–5 servings in the Vegetable Group
Examples of 1 serving are: 1 cup raw leafy vegetables; ½ cup cooked or chopped raw vegetables; ¾ cup vegetable juice.

• 2–4 servings in the Fruit Group
Examples of 1 serving are: 1 medium apple, banana, or orange; ½ cup chopped, cooked, or canned fruit; ¾ cup fruit juice.

At the next to the top layer of the pyramid, foods to be eaten in smaller quantities:
• 2–3 servings in the Milk, Yogurt, and Cheese Group
Examples of 1 serving are: 1 cup milk or yogurt; 1½ ounces natural cheese or 2 ounces processed cheese.

THE FOOD GUIDE PYRAMID—
Adapted for Vegetarian Cooking
A Guide to Daily Food Choices

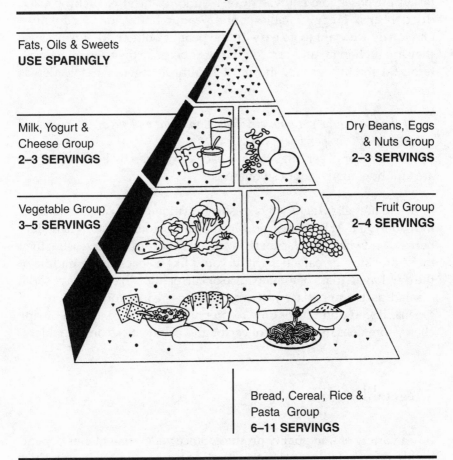

Fats, Oils & Sweets
USE SPARINGLY

Milk, Yogurt &
Cheese Group
2–3 SERVINGS

Dry Beans, Eggs
& Nuts Group
2–3 SERVINGS

Vegetable Group
3–5 SERVINGS

Fruit Group
2–4 SERVINGS

Bread, Cereal, Rice &
Pasta Group
6–11 SERVINGS

KEY

● Fat (naturally occurring and added)
▼ Sugars (added)

These symbols show fat and added sugars in foods. They come mostly from the fats, oils, and sweets group. But foods in other groups—such as cheese or ice cream from the milk group or french fries from the vegetable group—can also provide fat and added sugars.

Based on "The Food Guide Pyramid": U.S. Department of Agriculture/
U.S. Department of Health and Human Services.

• 2–3 servings in what is known as the Meat, Poultry, Fish, Dry Beans, Eggs & Nuts Group

Examples of 1 serving are: 2–3 ounces cooked meat, or, for vegetarian purposes, the equivalent of 1 ounce of meat is ½ cup cooked dried beans, 1 egg, 2 tablespoons peanut butter, or ⅓ cup nuts. Obviously we want to go easy on the peanut butter and nuts because they are high in fat and easy on the eggs because they contain cholesterol. So for this group, the most healthful vegetarian selection is beans.

At the peak of the pyramid are foods high in fat and sugar, which should be eaten as little as possible:
The number of servings to have each day varies by how active you are and how many calories you need.

There are all sorts of ways to slip nutritious fruits and vegetables into your diet. At breakfast, add fresh fruit to your cereal. When blueberries, strawberries, blackberries, and raspberries are in season, they make breakfast cereal a delight. If you'd like a snack in the middle of the day, have a glass of tomato juice or carrot juice. Try to always serve a salad as the appetizer of each meal, to ensure you eat plenty of greens. If you don't have time to prepare salad, place a bowl of ripe cherry tomatoes or a platter of carrot and celery sticks on the table.

Vegetables

Buy a variety of fine-quality produce. Since vegetarian menus depend highly on vegetables and fruits, starting with good tasting produce means you're more likely to have enjoyable meals.

Our markets are meeting the needs of busy cooks by providing a vast array of fresh, ready-to-use vegetables in bulk, in bags, and in microwave-safe trays. They have done a lot of the peeling, washing, and cutting for us. For many dishes, all you need do is open the bag, pour the vegetables directly into a salad bowl, add seasonings, and serve. Or put ready-to-cook vegetables in a pot, add water and flavorings, and briefly cook them.

Even in ordinary markets I now find cleaned spinach, diced onions, broccoli florets, and peeled carrots. Some stores feature peeled shrink-wrapped potatoes cut into fancy shapes, from ovals to little mushrooms! You can quickly steam them, microwave them, or use them in stews or sautés. Recently I found spaghetti squash removed from its shell and sold in "spaghetti" form, with a one-minute cooking time.

For salads and snacks, there is a growing variety of greens and other ingredients—plain and fancy lettuces, shredded cabbage, carrot and celery sticks, cleaned radishes, and many kinds of sprouts.

Use fresh vegetables as often as possible. Use the following liberally in your quick menus:

1. *Vegetables that are naturally easy to prepare and cook quickly:* broccoli, cauliflower, cabbage, zucchini, crookneck squash, pattypan or scallopini squash, baby squashes, Japanese eggplant, Swiss chard, green beans, sugar snap peas, button mushrooms, exotic mushrooms, cabbage, carrots.
2. *Easy to use salad vegetables:* tomatoes, cherry tomatoes, peppers, cucumbers, green onions, radishes, celery, jicama, bean sprouts, radish sprouts, lettuces, spinach, leafy herbs.
3. *Ready-cut and cleaned fresh vegetables:* shredded green and red cabbage (including cole slaw mix), cleaned spinach (regular and baby spinach leaves), rinsed lettuce, shredded lettuce, sliced mushrooms, diced onions, peeled garlic, broccoli florets, cauliflower florets, carrot sticks, peeled small carrots, shredded carrots, celery sticks, winter squash sticks, husked corn, asparagus, sugar snap peas.
4. *Frozen vegetables:* peas, corn, spinach, chopped collard greens and other greens, different combinations of mixed vegetables, sugar snap peas, snow peas, baby onions, asparagus spears, chopped onions, bell pepper strips.
5. *Vegetables in cans and in jars:* diced tomatoes (plain and seasoned with herbs), oil-packed sun-dried tomatoes, roasted peppers, diced chiles, water chestnuts, straw mushrooms, baby corn, corn kernels, beets, pumpkin, marinated artichokes, marinated mushrooms, pickled vegetables.
6. *Dried vegetables, for use as flavorings:* dry-packed sun-dried tomatoes, chiles, dried mushrooms, dried onions.

Beans

Beans and other legumes are important in vegetarian menus as a source of protein. For quick cooking, remember that:

1. Frozen lima beans and black-eyed peas are the fastest-cooking beans.
2. Packaged soaked beans, such as black-eyed peas and chickpeas, cook more quickly than their dried versions.
3. Lentils, split peas, and some quick-cooking dried beans, often packaged as bean soup or beans with other ingredients, cook rapidly. The soups can make a meal on their own if you serve them with good bread. Check the cooking instructions, though, because some packaged bean soups have long cooking times, while others require only 20 minutes.
4. Canned black beans, chickpeas, pinto beans, great northern and other white beans, red kidney beans, black-eyed peas, and butter beans (large lima beans) need only to be briefly heated. Try to buy plain beans. Read the labels to be sure the beans don't contain concealed fat. Also, beans in sauce are sometimes very high in sodium. Today you can also find Mexican-style refried beans in low-fat and nonfat versions.
5. Tofu, a special ingredient made from soybeans, is rich in nutrients. Now a low-fat version is available that is useful in low-fat vegetarian cooking. It is ready-to-eat and comes in four forms: soft, regular, firm, and extra-firm. Tofu takes on the flavors of the sauces or seasonings you use with it and is a satisfying addition to stews and soups.

Fruit

Fresh fruit is so enticing that it's easy to eat the recommended 2 to 4 servings a day. The sweet taste of fruit makes it a favorite of children and adults. When children come over to my house, they often go straight to the fruit bowl. This is a healthy habit that is worth encouraging, as fruits contribute vitamins C and A, minerals, and fiber to our diet. Enjoying each fruit at its peak and in its different varieties is a wonderful way to celebrate the seasons, with the selection of colorful items in your fruit bowl changing from one month to the next. Fortunately, there seems to be a greater and better array of fresh and prepared fruit each year, as market managers become more aware of the importance of fine quality produce.

1. *Fresh fruit.* Whether it's a crisp apple, a juicy peach, or a bowl of perfect strawberries, fresh fruit is the classic dessert or snack. Have plenty of citrus fruit, apples, bananas, and top-quality seasonal fruits on hand.
2. *Fresh prepared fruit.* Many markets offer peeled diced pineapple, halved melons, melon balls, halved papayas, and other fruits in their salad bar or in the prepared produce department.
3. *Frozen fruit.* Frozen berries and peaches can be quickly blended into tasty sauces and low-fat shakes.
4. *Fruit in cans and jars.* Applesauce is a terrific ingredient for creating low-fat desserts. Canned pineapple, lychees, and other tropical fruits can enhance fresh fruit salads.
5. *Dried fruit.* Dried fruits are good as snacks and add interest to breakfast cereal, sweet-and-sour main dishes, and desserts. Vary your pantry selection (and your recipes) with more than just raisins and prunes; there are dried cranberries, cherries, blueberries, currants, apricots, apples, and pears.

Juices and Other Beverages

Many Americans start the day with a glass of orange juice for breakfast. This healthful habit is a refreshing, easy way to get an early-morning nutritional boost of vitamin C.

But there's a wide variety of other fresh and canned fruits and vegetable juices at the market, from grapefruit to guava and from carrot to spinach. Those in the refrigerated section are freshest, but it's good to check the date on the container. Fresh juices make tasty, energy-restoring drinks at different times of the day and can also serve as meal enhancers. In addition, juices can lend interest to salad dressings, soups, stews, and desserts.

Be sure to read the labels on these beverages, however. Some canned vegetable juices contain large amounts of salt, but there are often lower-sodium versions available. Note that many fruit drinks contain only a small percentage of real fruit juice and quite a lot of sugar, and thus have much less nutritional benefit than pure juice.

For a light beverage, hot or iced tea is a good choice. Or select from a dizzying array of herbal teas, from apple to orange to raspberry.

Pasta

Pasta provides a fast foundation for a vegetarian entrée. I often cook some linguine, add some broccoli florets to the cooking water, then drain and top the mixture with diced tomato, basil leaves, and a trickle of extra-virgin olive oil or a very light sprinkling of grated Parmesan cheese. In the same way, you can combine pasta with other fresh or frozen vegetables to create easy, delicious main courses.

1. *Fresh pasta.* In the refrigerator and freezer section of your market, you can find low-cholesterol or no-yolk pasta, as well as tortellini and other stuffed pastas with meatless fillings. Reduced-fat versions of stuffed pastas are also available.
2. *Dried pasta.* Some forms of dried pasta, such as angel hair and linguine, can cook almost as rapidly as fresh pasta. Add interest to your meals by varying the shapes, colors, and flavors of pasta. Don't forget to use couscous, which looks like a grain but is in fact a practically instant pasta.

Note that some pasta cooks much more quickly than others. You can find packages of fettuccine that need 12 minutes of cooking, while others need only 2 minutes. Spaghetti's cooking times varies from 4 to 11 minutes. This makes a big difference in 30-minute meals. Check the times on the packages, and keep a good supply of the fastest-cooking ones on hand.

Pasta in a great variety of flavors is available both fresh and dried. Flavored pastas are time-savers because they already have seasoning. Many of them are eggless. Egg noodles used to be the selling point of good pasta, as "egg" suggested the finest noodles. Now, many pasta makers are offering flavor without egg, in such variations as tomato-basil pasta, red chile and jalapeño linguine, lemon-pepper noodles, and spinach-nutmeg fettuccine.

Remember to check the Asian products section of the market.

There is a wealth of quick-cooking noodles there, such as bright yellow Japanese chuka soba, which cooks in 1 or 2 minutes, and the fast-cooking clear noodles—rice vermicelli and bean threads. Some Asian noodles are available fresh; you can often find them in the refrigerated section of deli items.

Grains, Cereals, and Breads

These staples from the base of the USDA Food Pyramid are important in all diets, but especially in vegetarian ones. Like dried beans, some grains take a long time to cook, but today there are many time-saving options.

1. *Quick-cooking grains.* Besides white rice, try quick-cooking brown rice, bulgur wheat, buckwheat groats (also called kasha), and kashi (a mixture of quick-cooking grains). Vary your menus with jasmine rice and aromatic Basmati rice. In natural foods stores and some well-stocked supermarkets, you can find other grains, such as fast-cooking barley, amaranth, and quinoa.
2. *Hot cereals.* Oatmeal, cornmeal, cream of wheat, whole wheat cereal, and quick-cooking grits are nutritious and easy to prepare. Cereals are, in fact, grains and many cereals can appear in other meals besides breakfast, as side dishes or as thickeners for soups.
3. *Cold cereals.* Read the label on ready-to-eat cereals to choose those that are low in fat. Sweeten cereals with fresh and dried fruits instead of buying those that are high in sugar.
4. *Breads.* Good bread is an important part of any vegetarian diet. Together with a hearty soup or a substantial salad, it can make a meal. Buy the best bread you can find so you don't need to spread butter on it to make it taste good. Do read the label to be sure the bread doesn't contain hidden fat. Rye bread, bagels, and baguettes tend to be low in fat.
5. *Flat breads.* Use tortillas, pita breads, prepared crepes, and pizza bases with easy vegetable toppings to make main courses. The crepes also make easy desserts. Choose versions that are fat-free or low in fat.
6. *Crisp breads and crackers.* Bread sticks, bagel chips, crackers, and rice cakes can accompany soups, salads, and low-fat dips. Rice cakes

can also be used instead of bread to make canapés or other light appetizers. Many of these items are available in a variety of flavors. Rice cakes, for example, come in sesame, Cheddar, and apple cinnamon, to name a few. Their fat content can vary, so be sure to check the labels.

Dairy Products and Eggs

Dairy products are an important source of calcium and protein and are immensely useful in vegetarian cooking as they help make meals satisfying and delicious. Their uses in the kitchen are countless. A very light sprinkling of grated cheese adds a good deal of flavor to pasta, grains, vegetables, and soups. Milk gives vegetable soups and sauces a creamy texture and good taste. Nonfat sour cream and yogurt make great toppings for baked potatoes and other cooked vegetables and are also terrific with fresh or cooked fruits. I often finish a casual supper with diced oranges, peaches, or strawberries mixed with yogurt.

Eggs can be used occasionally in a healthful, low-fat diet. Although they are high in cholesterol, most of their fat is not saturated and they are a good source of protein. Adding an egg can turn a too-light meal into a substantial one. For example, a hard-boiled egg served warm with cooked vegetables and a bowl of brown rice makes a satisfying supper. For scrambled eggs and other dishes that contain beaten eggs, you can replace half or two thirds of the eggs with egg whites or egg substitute to lower the cholesterol. Be sure to cook eggs with little or no fat. If you're scrambling them, use a nonstick skillet and just a bit of oil spray.

1. *Low-fat dairy products.* Nonfat versions of sour cream, yogurt, milk, cream cheese, cottage cheese, and frozen yogurt, as well as light ice cream are useful in low- and nonfat vegetarian meals. Note that not all brands of nonfat sour cream and yogurt are created equal. Taste several brands to see which you prefer. If you don't like one company's product, it doesn't mean you won't find another one acceptable or even appealing. A tip for after-dinner delights: Ricotta cheese is good mixed with nonfat sour cream for making desserts.

2. *"Real" cheeses.* Because meatless menus tend to be low in satu-rated fat, occasionally you can accent your healthful menus with real cheeses like grated Parmesan, crumbled feta, or shredded Swiss cheese. Because these cheeses have plenty of flavor, a little goes a long way.
3. *Dairy substitutes.* If you prefer not to use dairy products, you can substitute rice milk or soy milk for regular milk in soups, desserts, and many other recipes; you can even find low-fat rice milk ice cream.
4. *Eggs.* Use eggs sparingly or combine them with egg substi-tutes—these are low in cholesterol and often low in fat, and some are pretty good.

Flavorings

Keep a good selection of seasonings on hand to quickly add flavor and zip to meals. Some examples are canned tomato sauce, canned vegetable broth, bottled Chinese sauces, good vinegars, mustards, capers, pickles, olive oil, walnut oil, sesame oil, low-fat mayonnaise, dried herbs, spices, and wine.

Dessert Ingredients

There is an increasing number of ingredients available for making tasty, low-fat desserts. Use sorbets and frozen fruits from the frozen foods department. Choose low-fat baked goods: angel food cake, sponge cake dessert cups, and ladyfingers. These can be combined with fruit and frozen yogurt to make sweet treats. And don't forget the cereal aisle. Granola, muesli, and other cereals make tasty sprin-kles for fruit topped with fat-free yogurt or sour cream, or for light ice cream desserts. Always read the labels and choose the low-fat ver-sions.

COOKING TECHNIQUES

Before beginning to cook, think for just a moment about how you'll proceed. Check the menu's game plan or develop your own, either mentally or in writing. First prepare the dishes that take longest to cook and those, such as grain dishes, that can tolerate standing for some time. Keep in mind that you can make a salad or dice the ingredients for a dish while another dish is simmering. Be organized. Take out the ingredients and utensils you'll need before you start cooking.

Boil and Simmer

These may not sound like exciting techniques, but they are among the most useful for getting vegetables cooked fast so they have good taste and texture. These cooking methods are also important for cooking pasta and grains, and are convenient for cooking vegetables and grains in the same pot.

To keep green vegetables bright green, add them to a saucepan of boiling salted water, using enough water to generously cover the vegetables. Boil the vegetables uncovered over high heat until they are crisp-tender. Drain them at once, and if you're not serving them immediately, rinse them with cold water.

Steam

Good for most vegetables, steaming takes a few minutes more than boiling, but keeps in more nutrients. Steaming is great for potatoes, beets, carrots, summer squashes, spinach, and other greens.

Poach in Sauce or Soup

Cook tender vegetables, such as zucchini, crookneck squash, and mushrooms, in sauces, especially tomato sauce, or in soups. This method imparts flavor to the vegetables, makes serving easy, and cuts down on the number of pots you use in cooking.

Broil and Grill

Use these techniques for cooking onions, eggplant, peppers, mushrooms, and tomatoes. You will use much less fat (or no fat) when broiling or grilling than when sautéing. Take advantage of these cooking methods to adapt old-fashioned recipes to low-fat cooking. For example, if you have an eggplant casserole that calls for frying the eggplant, grill it instead as in Grilled Eggplant Slices with Roasted Pepper Dressing (page 60), then proceed with your recipe.

To save time grilling, use a gas or stovetop grill rather than a charcoal grill, which takes a while to heat. Use a minimal amount of oil to keep the food moist and to oil the grill. Oil spray is useful for this.

Roast

Roasting is good for the same vegetables as broiling. Although roasting is not as quick as broiling, roasting time is often unattended time. Besides, you save work in cutting, because vegetables can be roasted whole or in large pieces. Use high temperatures to cook the vegetables rapidly.

Sauté and Stir-Fry

Sautéing and wok cooking are fast ways to cook many vegetables. Slice or dice the vegetables so they will cook evenly.

To gain time, heat the oil for sautéing over high heat. Be sure to use a sturdy pan and watch the oil so it doesn't burn. After you add the food, turn down the heat according to the recipe.

To make these techniques lower in fat, follow these guidelines:

- Use nonstick pans
- Sauté with a cover on to keep in moisture and help food cook without burning
- Use vegetable oil spray to use less oil

Quick-Braise

Choose this technique as an easy alternative to sautéing, as quick-braising needs less attention. First sauté the vegetables briefly in a bit of oil, then add a little broth, chopped tomatoes, or other liquid to finish cooking. This technique works well for eggplant, zucchini, onions, peppers, and mushrooms.

Microwave

The microwave is a great time-saver for cooking vegetables and expands the variety of vegetables you can add to 30-minute menus. For example, you can easily add nutritious sweet potatoes or butternut squash to your meal if you microwave them. The microwave is also convenient for cooking corn on the cob, white potatoes, asparagus, and frozen vegetables. You can use the microwave for quick "sautéing" of onions and peppers, and for making vegetable casseroles and pasta sauces. If you have cooked extra rice or other grains, the microwave reheats them quickly.

Like steaming, microwaving conserves the nutrients in vegetables better than boiling. Since little water is used for microwave cooking, you don't lose many vitamins into the cooking liquid. Besides, microwaving cooks the vegetables quickly, and this also helps them retain vitamins and minerals. If you are using salt, sprinkle it over the vegetables after microwaving them rather than before, for more even cooking.

Here are some additional ideas to make your low-fat meals quick to prepare.

Use Prepared Ingredients as Part of the Recipe

Many ready-to-eat or partly cooked ingredients can be of great help in quick cooking. Reduce the cooking time of soups and stews by using canned vegetable broth or packaged dry ingredients, such as 20-minute minestrone. With the broth or soup mix as a tasty base, you can have a fast, satisfying soup by adding frozen or diced fresh vegetables.

When you want something sweet, "assemble" desserts by combining fresh fruit with prepared low-fat ingredients. Top slices of angel food cake with raspberries and vanilla frozen yogurt. Use fresh or dried fruit with low-fat ice cream, frozen yogurt, sponge cake cups, and low-fat or fat-free cookies to put together quick desserts.

Make Quick Sauces from Tomatoes or Yogurt

Tomatoes, whether fresh or canned, cook down to pleasant-textured sauces that vary from chunky to smooth. Cook tomatoes briefly for a lively, fresh taste or longer for a deeper, richer-flavored sauce. Add tomato sauces to pasta, grain, bean, or vegetable dishes.

Yogurt is the easiest ingredient to make into sauce. You don't cook these sauces; simply stir the yogurt with flavorful ingredients such as minced garlic or fresh or dried herbs and spices, such as cumin, coriander, and cayenne pepper. Serve these sauces with hot or cold cooked vegetables, legumes, or grains.

Use Fresh Herbs the Easy Way

It might seem that fresh herbs have little place in quick cooking because of the time required to chop them, but actually, they don't have to be chopped. You can use them as sprigs. It's amazing how much a single sprig of fragrant fresh basil, for example, can do for a plate of plainly cooked beans and rice. And it's not just the aroma and the bright fresh appearance—the basil sprig makes a big difference in flavor. Just tear off bits of basil leaves (or cilantro, tarragon, or Italian parsley) and eat them with your rice and beans.

In several Asian cuisines it's the custom to put a tray of herbs on the table during meals. This is a good and useful idea. At dinner, each person can pull off leaves or small sprigs and sprinkle them over individual servings of salads, legumes, grains, or pasta. The herbs add a burst of fresh flavor and save you time because you don't need to chop them.

Prepare One-Pot Meals

Cook pasta, rice, or beans together with vegetables to save time in cooking, serving, and cleaning up. Add spices, herbs, and sauces and you will find that as the ingredients cook together, there will be a beneficial exchange of flavors.

Cook Extra Portions

When you cook grains, dried beans, long-cooking vegetables, or vegetable soups, it's a good idea to cook enough for two or more meals. In most cases, this involves little or no extra work, and that extra cooked rice or beans will be valuable for a later menu. Spoon the extra portions into containers that can go from the freezer to the microwave. These foods reheat beautifully.

Keep Your Kitchen Organized for Quick Cooking

Have your knives, cutting board, measuring cups, measuring spoons, wooden spoons, and a few useful saucepans in a convenient place, so you are encouraged to cook. When it's easy to get a meal started, you'll save time and energy preparing it.

Use Good-Quality Nonstick Pans

Heavy-duty nonstick pans enable you to cook with little or no fat. If you have sturdy pans, you can gain time by sautéing over higher heat without burning the food.

Use Time-Saving Equipment

Use your food processor often to chop onions, garlic, and fresh herbs and to shred cabbage, carrots, and other vegetables. For mincing small amounts of garlic or parsley, a mini food processor is convenient. Make delicious shakes, smoothies, and other dessert drinks in the blender. A blender or food processor is also great for pureeing soups and making quick dessert sauces from fruit.

CHAPTER 2

PASTA MENUS

A Springtime Pasta Dinner

• *Angel hair pasta with asparagus and sun-dried tomatoes* •
• *Salad of exotic mushrooms, baby lettuce, and toasted pecans* •
• *French bread* •
• *Strawberry-banana-orange medley with vanilla yogurt* •

AMOUNT OF CALORIES FROM FAT: **24%**

What better way to welcome spring than with this elegant menu, in which asparagus, the season's star, is paired with delicate fresh angel hair pasta. This pasta entrée makes use of the dry form of sun-dried tomatoes, which are less expensive than oil-packed dry tomatoes and have an extra bonus—they are fat-free. Thyme and a touch of extra-virgin olive oil complete the seasoning of this simple dish. The salad is also festive, with its quick-sautéed porcini mushrooms and baby greens dressed with walnut oil vinaigrette. For dessert, flavor the fruit with orange juice and honey, a delicious dressing for any fruit salad.

ALTERNATIVES:

⇨ Vary the main course by using flavored pasta. Lemon linguine or herbed fettuccine are good partners for the asparagus.

⇨ Instead of sun-dried tomatoes, toss the pasta with diced canned tomatoes or roasted red peppers from a jar.

⇨ For a faster version of the salad, top the lettuce with enoki mushrooms, canned straw mushrooms, or sliced white mushrooms (or some of each) instead of sautéed portabello mushrooms. In this case, omit the vegetable oil.

⇨ If you prefer a vegan menu, serve the fruit in its orange-honey sauce without the yogurt.

GAME PLAN:

Step 1. Boil water for pasta.
Step 2. Toast pecans.
Step 3. Cut asparagus.
Step 4. Prepare dessert; refrigerate fruit and yogurt.
Step 5. Cook for salad and pasta simultaneously:
    A. Sauté mushrooms for salad.
    B. Cook tomatoes and asparagus; prepare oregano mixture.
Step 6. Toss lettuce with dressing.
Step 7. Finish pasta.

TIPS:

♥ There are flavored nonfat yogurts on the market that you can use to top fruit, but often they have excessive amounts of sugar or sweetener. I prefer the natural flavor of plain nonfat yogurt and I add pure vanilla extract to taste.

! Buy pencil-thin asparagus—it cooks fastest and there's no need to peel it.

⊕ Some markets sell asparagus spears with their bottoms already trimmed. Ready-to-cook asparagus spears are often available in microwave-safe trays.

⊕ Angel hair pasta cooks very quickly, even from the frozen state.

ANGEL HAIR PASTA WITH ASPARAGUS AND SUN-DRIED TOMATOES

1½ pounds thin asparagus
20 dry-packed sun-dried tomatoes
1 teaspoon dried oregano
3 tablespoons extra-virgin olive oil
Salt and freshly ground pepper
2 (9-ounce) packages fresh angel hair pasta

Cut off bottom inch of each asparagus stalk. Cut each asparagus spear diagonally into 3 pieces.

Put dried tomatoes in a large pot of boiling water. Boil 2 minutes. Add asparagus. Boil 3 minutes. Meanwhile, in a large bowl, combine oregano, olive oil, salt, and pepper. Add pasta to pot of asparagus. Boil 1 minute or until pasta is tender but still firm to the bite. Drain pasta and vegetables. Transfer mixture to bowl of seasoning mixture. Toss well using tongs. Taste and adjust seasoning. Serve as soon as possible.

Makes 4 servings.

SALAD OF EXOTIC MUSHROOMS, BABY LETTUCE, AND TOASTED PECANS

¼ *cup pecan halves*
1 (6-ounce) package sliced portabello mushrooms or other fresh
  exotic mushrooms
1 tablespoon vegetable oil
Salt and freshly ground pepper
1½ tablespoons walnut oil
2 teaspoons wine vinegar or herb vinegar
6 cups mixed baby lettuces

Preheat toaster oven or oven to 350°F. Toast pecans in oven for 5 minutes.

Cut large whole mushrooms into bite-size pieces. If using sliced portabellos, you can leave the slices whole. In a medium nonstick skillet, heat vegetable oil. Add mushrooms, salt, and pepper and sauté over medium-high heat about 5 minutes or until tender and browned.

In a small bowl, whisk walnut oil, vinegar, salt, and pepper. In a serving bowl, toss lettuce with vinaigrette. Taste and adjust seasoning. Serve lettuce topped with mushrooms. Sprinkle with toasted pecans.

Makes 4 servings.

STRAWBERRY-BANANA-ORANGE MEDLEY WITH VANILLA YOGURT

1 tablespoon honey
2 tablespoons orange juice
2 medium bananas
1 large orange
1 pint strawberries, hulled and quartered
1½ cups plain nonfat yogurt
1½ teaspoons vanilla extract

Mix honey and orange juice in a serving bowl. Peel and slice bananas; add to bowl. Cut peel from orange. Divide orange into segments and cut them in half. Add orange segments and strawberries to bowl. Mix gently. Refrigerate until ready to serve.

In a cup, mix yogurt and vanilla. Serve fruit topped with vanilla yogurt.

Makes 4 servings.

A Summer Supper from Southern Italy

- *Spinach salad with chickpeas and peppers* •
- *Rotini with zucchini, tomatoes, and basil* •
- *Vanilla ice cream with fresh blackberry sauce* •

—————— AMOUNT OF CALORIES FROM FAT: **23%** ——————

This menu is inspired by a lunch my husband and I enjoyed at a small trattoria in the beautiful town of Amalfi, on the southwestern coast of Italy. We feasted on fusilli in a garlic-scented zucchini sauce, followed by veal scallopini with lightly cooked spinach. The spinach was served the traditional Italian way, accompanied by fresh lemon wedges and a small cruet of olive oil. Dessert was a lovely *coppa di more*, a wide glass filled with luscious blackberries topped with vanilla ice cream.

Back home in Los Angeles, I created a vegetarian menu in the spirit of that lovely meal. For the colorful appetizer, I combined packaged cleaned spinach leaves with strips of red or yellow peppers and moistened the salad with a dressing of fresh lemon juice, olive oil, and oregano. I cooked the wheel-shaped pasta and the zucchini in one pot, then tossed both with a super-quick tomato sauce seasoned with garlic and hot pepper flakes. Low-fat vanilla ice cream topped with an easy sauce of strawberry jelly heated with fresh blackberries made a lively, guilt-free dessert. Instead of serving dessert, you might like to follow a popular Italian custom: bring a big bowl of cool, fresh seasonal fruit such as plums, peaches, apricots, and grapes to the table.

ALTERNATIVES:

⇨ Use romaine lettuce instead of spinach in the salad.
⇨ Prepare a quicker version of the rotini dish by substituting fresh angel hair pasta.
⇨ Substitute broccoli florets for the zucchini.
⇨ Prepare the dessert sauce with half blackberries and half raspberries.

GAME PLAN:

Step 1. Boil water for pasta.
Step 2. Cut zucchini, tomatoes, garlic, and basil for pasta dish.
Step 3. Prepare salad, vegetables, and dressing.
Step 4. Prepare sauce for dessert.
Step 5. Finish salad and pasta.

TIPS:

♥ Make your favorite ice cream desserts with fat-free frozen yogurt or light ice cream, for a substantial reduction of fat.
① To make almost instant sauces for pasta, use canned diced tomatoes. For this menu, choose plain or Italian-flavored tomatoes.
① Substitute vinegar for lemon juice in salad dressings. Vinegar is faster because you avoid the steps of squeezing and straining the juice.

Spinach Salad with Chickpeas and Peppers

1 large red bell pepper
4 cups spinach leaves, medium packed
1 (8¾-ounce) can chickpeas (garbanzo beans), drained
1½ tablespoons extra-virgin olive oil or vegetable oil
2 teaspoons balsamic vinegar or lemon juice
¼ teaspoon dried oregano
Salt and freshly ground pepper

Quarter pepper lengthwise around core. Cut pepper pieces in cross-wise strips about ⅓ inch wide; cut in half if long. Combine with spinach and chickpeas in a large bowl.

In a small bowl, whisk oil with vinegar and oregano. Add to salad and toss. Season to taste with salt and pepper.

Makes 4 servings.

Rotini with Zucchini, Tomatoes, and Basil

1 pound small zucchini
8 ounces rotini, fusilli, or other spiral pasta
2 tablespoons extra-virgin olive oil
1 small garlic clove, minced
Salt and freshly ground pepper
1 pound ripe tomatoes, diced, or 1 (14½-ounce) can diced
    tomatoes, drained
¼ to ½ teaspoon hot red pepper flakes
¼ cup basil leaves, cut into strips

Halve zucchini lengthwise, set cut side down, and halve lengthwise again. Cut each piece in 2-inch lengths.

Cook pasta uncovered in a large pot of boiling salted water over high heat, stirring occasionally, 5 minutes. Add zucchini and boil 3 minutes or until pasta is tender but firm to the bite. Drain in colander.

Meanwhile, in a large bowl, combine oil, garlic, salt, and pepper.

To pot used in cooking pasta, add tomatoes and hot pepper flakes and cook over medium heat about 2 minutes. Add to bowl of garlic mixture. Add pasta and zucchini and toss thoroughly. Taste and adjust seasoning. Serve topped with basil.

Makes 4 servings.

VANILLA ICE CREAM WITH FRESH BLACKBERRY SAUCE

⅓ cup strawberry jelly
1 (6-ounce) basket fresh blackberries (about 1⅓ cups)
1 tablespoon raspberry brandy or fruit liqueur (optional)
4 to 8 scoops nonfat or reduced-fat vanilla ice cream or frozen yogurt

Melt jelly over low heat. Remove from heat and stir in blackberries. Reheat gently before serving. Remove from heat and add brandy. Serve warm over ice cream.

Makes 4 servings.

Dinner for a Busy Weekend

• *White bean and beet salad* •
• *Noodles with cauliflower and Hungarian pepper sauce* •
• *No-cook fruit soup* •

AMOUNT OF CALORIES FROM FAT: **19%**

Here's a weekend menu in the style of Eastern Europe. The first course pairs a regional favorite—beets—with beans and fresh greens. Save yourself the trouble of cooking beets and slipping off their peels under running water. Now beets are beginning to be sold in the produce sections of our markets as conveniently as in Europe—freshly cooked and peeled. All you do is slice them and add them to the salad. Canned beets of good quality are even easier to find, and you can substitute either the sliced or the julienned form.

For the pasta entrée, the sauce is adapted from a pepper stew called *lecso* that traditionally calls for bacon and lard. I omit the meats for a lighter, more healthful result; instead, I sauté the onions, green peppers, and tomatoes in a little vegetable oil and accent the sauce with cayenne pepper.

Soups of cooked fruit are favorites throughout the region. Our dessert is a refreshing cold soup of seasonal fruit in red wine, but the fruit is not cooked so it retains its texture and fresh flavor. Even on a hectic weekend, you can easily fit this menu into your schedule. You can make the dessert and the sauce for the noodles ahead and have the salad nearly assembled, so that dinner can be ready when you need it.

ALTERNATIVES:

⇨ In winter, substitute bananas and ripe pears for the peaches and berries in the fruit soup.

⇨ Use baby lettuce or bite-size pieces of green leaf lettuce instead of romaine lettuce.

GAME PLAN:

Step 1. Boil water for noodles.
Step 2. Prepare pepper sauce; cut cauliflower.
Step 3. Prepare fruit soup.
Step 4. Prepare salad.
Step 5. Cook noodles and cauliflower.

TIPS:

♥ You can find low-sodium canned beans in the diet products or natural foods department of your supermarket or in health food stores.

☺ Canned beets are widely available whole, sliced, and julienned. Some markets also carry fresh-cooked beets in their produce section. Note that some canned beets are pickled and have a different flavor.

☺ To save time, buy 4 or 5 cups prepared fresh cauliflower florets, or use frozen ones.

BEAN AND BEET SALAD

1 (15-ounce) can great northern or other white beans, drained
1½ tablespoons vegetable oil
2 teaspoons herb or white wine vinegar
Salt and freshly ground pepper
4 cups bite-size pieces romaine lettuce
1 (8-ounce) can shoestring or julienne-cut beets, drained, or
    8 ounces packaged cooked beets, diced

In a large serving bowl, mix beans, oil, vinegar, salt, and pepper. At serving time, mix lettuce with beans. Top with beets.

Makes 4 servings.

NOODLES WITH CAULIFLOWER AND HUNGARIAN PEPPER SAUCE

3 medium green bell peppers
1½ tablespoons vegetable oil
1 medium onion, halved and thinly sliced
2 teaspoons paprika
1 (14½-ounce) can diced tomatoes, drained
Salt and freshly ground pepper
Pinch of hot paprika or cayenne (optional)
1 medium head cauliflower, divided into small florets
8 ounces medium-wide noodles

Cut peppers into lengthwise strips about ½ inch wide and 2 to 3 inches long.

Heat oil in a medium sauté pan or skillet. Add onion and peppers and sauté over medium heat 3 minutes. Stir in paprika, then tomatoes, salt, and pepper. Cover and simmer over medium-low heat, stirring occasionally, about 10 minutes or until peppers are tender and sauce is thick. Taste and adjust seasoning; add hot paprika if desired.

Add cauliflower and noodles to a large pot of boiling salted water, and boil 5 to 7 minutes or until noodles are tender but still firm to the bite, al dente. Drain noodles and cauliflower, transfer to a large serving bowl, and toss with the sauce. Serve as soon as possible.

Makes 4 servings.

No-Cook Fruit Soup

1 cup orange juice
1 cup dry red wine, such as Cabernet Sauvignon
⅓ cup sugar
3 large ripe peaches or nectarines
1 cup raspberries, blackberries, or halved small strawberries
1 large orange

In a glass bowl, mix orange juice, wine, ¼ cup water, and sugar until sugar dissolves. Slice peaches or nectarines and add them to bowl. Add berries.

Peel orange, removing as much as possible of white pith. Cut into segments and cut segments in half. Add to bowl. Refrigerate 10 minutes or until ready to serve. Serve cold.

Makes 4 servings.

A Fast Couscous Feast

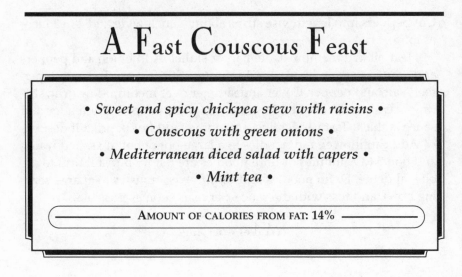

• *Sweet and spicy chickpea stew with raisins* •
• *Couscous with green onions* •
• *Mediterranean diced salad with capers* •
• *Mint tea* •

———— Amount of calories from fat: **14%** ————

Of Moroccan inspiration, this meal is so delicious that nobody would believe it's so easy to prepare and so low in fat. It is built around couscous, a tiny-grain pasta that is a staple in North Africa. Our couscous gains flavor from vegetable broth and is dotted with bright green flecks of scallion. I like to serve it the way I often enjoyed it at couscous eateries in Paris—with a satisfying casserole of chickpeas in a hot and garlicky tomato sauce. Add zip to the traditional Mediterranean chopped salad of tomatoes, cucumbers, and parsley by accenting it with capers. End the meal in the time-honored Moroccan way: with tea flavored with fresh mint leaves. In summer you might also like to serve fresh, vitamin A–rich apricots or juicy peaches.

ALTERNATIVES:

➪ Use black-eyed peas instead of chickpeas in the stew.
➪ Use whole wheat couscous, which is available at health food stores, instead of regular couscous; or substitute bulgur wheat or quick-cooking brown rice for the couscous.
➪ Instead of canned vegetable broth, you can use powdered vegetable broth with 1¾ cups water.

GAME PLAN:

Step 1. Prepare chickpea stew.
Step 2. Prepare couscous.
Step 3. Prepare salad.
Step 4. Prepare tea.

TIPS:

♥ Enrich couscous with a single tablespoon of canola oil instead of using butter. Oil goes further because it's fluid, and canola oil is the least saturated.

⊙ Couscous is the fastest cooking pasta. It's ready in 5 minutes, and you don't need to boil a big pot of water to cook it.

⊙ Use a mini food processor to quickly chop the garlic.

⊙ Dice tomatoes after cutting herbs and onions, as tomatoes make the board wet and then it's difficult to chop herbs and other vegetables efficiently.

SWEET AND SPICY CHICKPEA STEW WITH RAISINS

1 tablespoon olive or vegetable oil
4 large garlic cloves, chopped
1 (14½-ounce) can diced tomatoes, drained
1 (8-ounce) can tomato sauce
1½ teaspoons ground cumin
Salt and freshly ground pepper
½ teaspoon bottled hot sauce, or more to taste
2 (15-ounce) cans chickpeas (garbanzo beans), drained
⅓ cup raisins

Heat oil in a medium saucepan, add garlic, and sauté 10 seconds over medium heat. Add tomatoes, tomato sauce, cumin, salt, and pepper. Stir and bring to boil over high heat. Simmer uncovered over medium heat for 3 minutes. Stir in hot sauce, chickpeas, and raisins. Bring to a simmer. Cook uncovered over medium-low heat 5 minutes. Taste and adjust seasoning. Serve hot.

Makes 4 servings.

Couscous with Green Onions

1 (14½-ounce) can vegetable broth (1¾ cups)
1 tablespoon canola or other vegetable oil
4 green onions, sliced ¼ inch thick
1 (10-ounce) package couscous (1⅔ cups)

Combine broth, oil, and ¼ cup water in a medium saucepan and bring to a boil. Stir in green onions and return to boil. Stir in couscous, remove from heat, and let stand 5 minutes. Fluff with a fork before serving.

Makes 4 servings.

MEDITERRANEAN DICED SALAD WITH CAPERS

2 large or 4 small ripe tomatoes, diced (2 cups)
1 medium cucumber, peeled and diced (about 1⅔ cups)
½ large yellow or red bell pepper, diced
2 tablespoons chopped Italian parsley (optional)
2 teaspoons lemon juice
4 teaspoons extra-virgin olive oil
Salt and freshly ground pepper
2 teaspoons capers

Mix tomatoes, cucumber, bell pepper, parsley, lemon juice, and oil in a glass bowl. Season to taste with salt and pepper. Serve sprinkled with capers.

Makes 4 servings.

MINT TEA

2 to 4 Orange Pekoe tea bags, or tea of your preference
Sugar or sweetener to taste (optional)
4 fresh mint sprigs

Use clear mugs or glasses to make the tea so you see the mint. Prepare tea with boiling water in 4 glasses and sweeten it to your taste. Add a mint sprig to each glass. Serve hot.

Makes 4 servings.

Pasta for Two

• *Antipasto salad* •
• *Linguine with confetti vegetable sauce* •
• *Strawberries and blueberries with kirsch* •

AMOUNT OF CALORIES FROM FAT: **24%**

This savory, colorful menu illustrates a variety of shortcuts for planning meals. Prepare a fast, delectable sauce for pasta with both fresh and frozen vegetables. Use the microwave to quickly sauté onions, and cook mushrooms and garlic as the basis for a tasty sauce for the linguine. Complete the sauce, still using the microwave, by cooking a packaged medly of corn, broccoli, and red pepper with the sauce. This way you have pasta, sauce, and vegetables all in one dish. For an appetizer, liven up the usual tomato and lettuce salad by topping it with ingredients from your pantry—marinated artichokes and black olives.

ALTERNATIVES:

➪ In the antipasto salad, substitute strips of roasted peppers from a jar or oil-packed sun-dried tomatoes for the olives; or substitute marinated mushrooms for the artichokes.
➪ Add fresh whole basil leaves to the salad greens; they'll contribute a pleasing aroma and flavor.
➪ Serve the berries with vanilla yogurt or frozen yogurt; or to keep this menu vegan, serve the berries with rice milk ice cream.

GAME PLAN:

Step 1. Boil water for pasta.
Step 2. Prepare sauce for pasta.
Step 3. Prepare dessert.
Step 4. Prepare salad.
Step 5. Cook linguine; mix with sauce.

TIPS:

♥ Choose no-yolk pasta or low-cholesterol pasta.
☺ The microwave saves the most time when you're cooking small amounts, especially for 1 or 2 portions.

ANTIPASTO SALAD

3 cups bite-size pieces mixed lettuces or romaine lettuce
1 tablespoon extra-virgin olive oil
1½ teaspoons red wine vinegar
¼ teaspoon dried oregano
Salt and freshly ground pepper
1 large tomato, cut into wedges
4 pieces marinated artichokes (quarters)
4 black olives

In a shallow serving bowl, toss lettuce with oil, vinegar, and oregano. Season to taste with salt and pepper. Serve salad topped with tomato wedges, artichoke pieces, and olives.

Makes 2 servings.

LINGUINE WITH CONFETTI VEGETABLE SAUCE

1 medium onion, halved and sliced
2 tablespoons extra-virgin olive oil
1 large garlic clove, chopped
1 (16-ounce) package frozen corn, broccoli, and red pepper medley
6 medium mushrooms, thickly sliced
½ teaspoon dried thyme
1 (9-ounce) package fresh cholesterol-free linguine
Salt and freshly ground pepper

Boil a large pot of water for cooking linguine.

Combine onion and 1 tablespoon oil in 2-quart microwave-safe casserole. Cover and microwave on HIGH 3 minutes. Add garlic, top with frozen vegetables, cover, and microwave 4 minutes. Stir, add mushrooms, and sprinkle them with thyme. Cover and microwave about 3 more minutes or until vegetables are tender.

Cook linguine in boiling water about 2 minutes or according to package directions. Drain; add remaining 1 tablespoon oil and season to taste with salt and pepper. Serve topped with the vegetable sauce.

Makes 2 servings.

STRAWBERRIES AND BLUEBERRIES WITH KIRSCH

1 cup strawberries, quartered
1 cup blueberries
2 teaspoons sugar
2 teaspoons kirsch (clear cherry brandy)

Combine berries in a serving bowl. Sprinkle with sugar and kirsch, and mix gently using a rubber spatula. Cover and refrigerate 15 minutes or until ready to serve.

Makes 2 servings.

CHAPTER 3

BEAN MENUS

A French-Inspired Dinner

- *Black beans bourguignonne* •
- *Provençal rice with tricolor peppers* •
- *Butter lettuce with mustard vinaigrette* •
- *Chocolate orange coupe* •

AMOUNT OF CALORIES FROM FAT: **19%**

Whenever we prepared *boeuf bourguignonne* at La Varenne Cooking School in Paris, my favorite part was the savory mushrooms and baby onions in their luscious brown sauce. Since it was actually the vegetables that I loved best, I developed a vegetarian version of the dish. Black beans made a perfect substitute for the beef, as their rich flavor stands up to the hearty wine sauce. The meatless rendition is much easier and lighter than the classic. You simply heat the beans with red wine, vegetable broth, sautéed quartered mushrooms, baby onions, and herbs. Their colorful accompaniment is a rice pilaf embellished with strips of red, green, and yellow peppers, which are now available frozen. For a finale, enjoy a spirited French-style sundae of oranges sprinkled with orange liqueur and served around your favorite light chocolate ice cream or frozen yogurt.

ALTERNATIVES:

⇨ Instead of butter lettuce, use a combination of packaged butter lettuce and radicchio for a more colorful "green" salad.
⇨ Another good rice accompaniment for the beans is Basmati Rice with Vegetables and Cilantro (page 52), with Italian parsley substituted for the cilantro.

GAME PLAN:

Step 1. Begin cooking rice.
Step 2. Prepare beans.
Step 3. Add peppers to rice and finish cooking.
Step 4. Prepare oranges for dessert; refrigerate.
Step 5. Prepare salad dressing; toss salad at serving time.

TIPS

♥ Substitute beans for meat in traditional dishes to cut the fat drastically yet still have a satisfying entrée.
♥ Emulate the time-honored French tradition of serving a green salad after the main course. It's a healthful custom.
⊙ Frozen baby onions are a double time-saver: their cooking time is shorter than fresh and, best of all, they are already peeled!

BLACK BEANS BOURGUIGNONNE

1 tablespoon vegetable oil
8 ounces mushrooms, quartered
Salt and freshly ground pepper
⅓ cup dry red wine
¼ cup canned vegetable broth
1 bay leaf
½ teaspoon dried thyme
1 (10-ounce) package frozen baby onions
2 (15-ounce) cans black beans (canned with water and salt)
2 tablespoons chopped fresh parsley

Heat oil in a medium saucepan. Add mushrooms, sprinkle with salt and pepper, and sauté over medium-high heat 2 minutes. Add wine, broth, bay leaf, and thyme and bring to a boil. Add baby onions, cover, and return to a boil. Simmer over low heat about 10 minutes or until onions are tender. Add black beans and bring to a simmer over medium-high heat. Simmer uncovered 3 minutes. Discard bay leaf. Season beans to taste with salt and pepper. Serve sprinkled with parsley.

Makes 4 servings.

PROVENÇAL RICE WITH TRICOLOR PEPPERS

1 (1-pound) package frozen bell pepper strips (about 2½ cups)
1 tablespoon vegetable oil
1 medium onion, chopped (¾ cup)
1½ cups long-grain white rice
3 cups hot water
Salt and freshly ground pepper
½ teaspoon dried oregano

Remove pepper strips from freezer. Heat oil in a large, heavy sauté pan over medium heat. Add onion and sauté 3 minutes. Add rice and sauté, stirring, 1 minute. Pour hot water over rice and stir once. Add salt and pepper. Bring to boil over high heat. Cover and cook over low heat 10 minutes. Sprinkle pepper strips over top of rice; spread in an even layer but do not stir. Sprinkle with oregano. Cover and cook over low heat 10 minutes or until rice is tender, liquid is absorbed, and peppers are hot. Fluff rice with a fork. Taste and adjust seasoning.

Makes 4 servings.

BUTTER LETTUCE WITH MUSTARD VINAIGRETTE

1 teaspoon Dijon mustard
2 teaspoons wine vinegar or herb vinegar
Salt and freshly ground pepper
2 tablespoons vegetable oil
6 cups butter lettuce, or mixed butter lettuce and radicchio

In a small bowl, whisk mustard with vinegar, salt, and pepper. Whisk in oil. Just before serving, toss lettuce with dressing in a salad bowl. Taste and adjust seasoning.

Makes 4 servings.

CHOCOLATE ORANGE COUPE

2 large oranges
5 teaspoons Grand Marnier
4 scoops chocolate frozen yogurt or low-fat chocolate ice cream

Cut peel from oranges, removing most of white pith. Divide orange into segments, reserving any juice that escapes. Put orange segments and reserved juice in a bowl and sprinkle with Grand Marnier. Cover and refrigerate until ready to serve. At serving time, scoop frozen yogurt into dessert dishes and surround with orange segments and their juices.

Makes 4 servings.

An Easy Chili Fiesta

• Vegetarian chili in a hurry •
• Hot tortillas, country bread, or pita bread •
• Broccoli slaw with herb dressing •
• Guilt-free banana split •

AMOUNT OF CALORIES FROM FAT: 21%

Vegetarian chili can be as satisfying as chili with meat. Our low-fat chili has two surprise ingredients: chopped mushrooms to give it a meaty texture and a bit of soy sauce to deepen its color. Pinto beans, tomatoes, and chili spices complete the entrée and its cooking time is only about 15 minutes! It's great on its own or topped with a dollop of nonfat sour cream or a sprinkling of chopped cilantro, green onions, or hot salsa. You might also like to microwave some corn on the cob as an accompaniment. Follow the chili with a new version of everybody's favorite—banana split. By using nonfat ice creams and chocolate syrup, you eliminate the fat but still have plenty of flavor.

ALTERNATIVES:

⇨ For a milder chili, use ¼ teaspoon hot red pepper flakes and 1 teaspoon chili powder.

⇨ Make black bean chili; or use lima beans for a green and red chili.

⇨ Add 1 cup frozen pepper strips to the chili along with the tomatoes.

⇨ Add diced avocado or grated Cheddar or Monterey Jack cheese to the toppings, but use them with a light hand, as they add quite a bit of fat. Or use reduced-fat or nonfat cheese.

⇨ Use cole slaw mix instead of broccoli slaw.

GAME PLAN:

Step 1. Prepare chili.
Step 2. Prepare salad.
Step 3. Measure ingredients for dessert; assemble at serving time.

TIPS:

♥ Remember chocolate syrup for making desserts—the ordinary kind has only a little fat. You can also buy completely fat-free versions.

☺ Use ready-chopped onions for sautéing to save on time and tears!

☺ If using the food processor to chop vegetables and herbs, chop the onions after the garlic, mushrooms, and herbs because onions tend to make the processor wet.

☺ Use a sauté pan or wide casserole to cook chili so it thickens faster.

VEGETARIAN CHILI
IN A HURRY

4 large garlic cloves
1 (6-ounce) package sliced mushrooms
1 large onion, cut into 8 pieces
2 tablespoons olive or vegetable oil
2 teaspoons chili powder
2 teaspoons ground cumin
1½ teaspoons dried leaf oregano, crumbled
½ teaspoon hot red pepper flakes, or to taste
1 (28-ounce) can diced tomatoes, with their juice
2 (15- or 16-ounce) cans pinto beans or pink beans, drained
1 tablespoon soy sauce

Chop garlic in food processor. Add mushrooms and chop together using on-off pulses; remove. Chop onion in processor.

Heat oil in a wide casserole, stew pan, or Dutch oven. Add onion and sauté over medium heat, stirring often, 3 minutes. Add mushroom-garlic mixture. Sauté, stirring often, 3 minutes. Add chili powder, cumin, oregano, and pepper flakes and stir over low heat for ½ minute. Add tomatoes, stir, and bring to a boil over high heat. Add beans and soy sauce, and bring to a simmer. Simmer uncovered over medium heat 5 minutes, then over medium-high heat 3 minutes or until mixture is thick. Taste and adjust seasoning. Serve hot.

Makes 4 servings.

BROCCOLI SLAW WITH HERB DRESSING

2 tablespoons extra-virgin olive oil
2 tablespoons tarragon vinegar or herb vinegar
¼ teaspoon dried oregano or thyme
1 (1-pound) package broccoli slaw (shredded broccoli stems, carrots, and red cabbage) (6 cups)
Salt and freshly ground pepper

In a small bowl, whisk oil with vinegar and oregano. Toss with broccoli slaw mix. Season to taste with salt and pepper.

Makes 4 servings.

Guilt-Free Banana Split

4 tablespoons strawberry jelly or preserves
4 medium bananas
4 scoops vanilla nonfat ice cream or frozen yogurt
4 scoops chocolate or strawberry nonfat ice cream or frozen
   yogurt
2 tablespoons fat-free chocolate syrup
4 maraschino cherries (optional)

Heat jelly in a very small saucepan over low heat to soften. For each serving, peel and halve a banana and set pieces in a dessert dish, if possible oval or oblong shaped. Put a scoop of vanilla and a scoop of chocolate or strawberry ice cream in each dish. Spoon ½ tablespoon chocolate syrup over each serving of vanilla ice cream and 1 tablespoon jelly over the chocolate or strawberry ice cream. Top each serving with a maraschino cherry.

Makes 4 servings.

Tofu with an Indian Accent

• *Tandoori tofu* •
• *Basmati rice with vegetables and cilantro* •
• *Sliced cucumbers, tomatoes, and shredded lettuce* •
• *Mango milkshake* •

——————— AMOUNT OF CALORIES FROM FAT: **19%** ———————

You might already know that food from India can be rich in oil and ghee (clarified butter), but it doesn't have to be; it can be delectable with a minimal amount of oil. In this menu, a flavorful, spicy tandoori marinade typically used for poultry and meats imparts flavor and warm golden color to the tofu. Tofu is high in protein and is a satisfying meat substitute, yet it contains no cholesterol and is low in saturated fat. Although tofu is not low in total fat, when served with rice and vegetables, as in this menu, it fits nicely into low-fat menus. Besides, a new, low-fat tofu is now available in good supermarkets. The tofu's accompaniment, aromatic Basmati rice, has a fabulous taste cooked just plain, but for a nutritional boost and a pleasing crunchy texture, here it cooks with shredded carrots, cabbage, and frozen peas. The dessert is an easy version of a popular Indian smoothie or shake, called *lassi*.

ALTERNATIVES:

⇨ When you have more time, you can use brown Basmati rice, which takes 40 to 45 minutes to cook but has a lovely aroma and good flavor. When preparing it, cook extra for future meals. You can also prepare the rice dish with Texmati rice or regular long-grain white rice.

⇨ Instead of mango, use a 1-pound package of frozen peaches to make the milkshake. Increase the sugar to 5 tablespoons.

GAME PLAN:

Step 1. Cook rice.
Step 2. Marinate tofu.
Step 3. Remove mango (for dessert) and peas (for rice)
    from freezer.
Step 4. Finish tofu recipe.
Step 5. Prepare raw vegetables to serve on side.
Step 6. Prepare mango shake at serving time.

TIPS:

♥ Basmati rice is so delicious that it needs very little or no oil to enrich it.

☺ Tofu is ready to eat. It needs "cooking" only to heat it or blend flavors.

TANDOORI TOFU

1 (10.5-ounce) package firm low-fat tofu
2 large garlic cloves, minced
2 tablespoons vegetable oil
1 cup plain nonfat yogurt
2 teaspoons ground cumin
2 teaspoons ground coriander
2 teaspoons ground ginger
1 teaspoon turmeric
¼ teaspoon cayenne pepper
½ teaspoon salt
1 large onion, chopped, or 1 cup packaged diced onion
Oil spray (for coating broiler)
1 teaspoon paprika

Pat tofu dry between paper towels. In a bowl, mix garlic, 1 tablespoon oil, yogurt, cumin, coriander, ginger, turmeric, cayenne pepper, and salt. Add tofu and turn over to coat with marinade. Let stand 5 minutes. Meanwhile, heat remaining 1 tablespoon oil in a skillet, add onion, and sauté over medium heat or until onion begins to turn golden.

Preheat broiler with rack about 3 inches from heat. Line broiler pan with foil and lightly coat the foil with oil spray. Remove tofu from marinade, reserving marinade. Halve tofu horizontally and set in the prepared pan. Spoon a little marinade over each piece. Broil tofu for 2 minutes. Turn pieces over carefully, spoon a little more marinade over them, and broil about 2 minutes or until tofu is heated through and dotted with brown. Add remaining marinade to pan of onion and heat through, stirring. Do not boil. Stir in paprika. Serve tofu with sauce.

Makes 4 servings.

BASMATI RICE WITH VEGETABLES AND CILANTRO

1½ cups white Basmati rice, rinsed and drained
3 cups hot water
1 tablespoon vegetable oil
Salt and freshly ground pepper
1⅓ cups frozen peas
1 cup shredded cabbage or cole slaw mix
1½ cups shredded carrots
Small cilantro sprigs or leaves

FAYE LEVY

Combine rice, hot water, oil, and salt and pepper to taste in a large saucepan. Bring to a boil over high heat. Boil 1 minute. Reduce heat to low, cover tightly, and simmer without stirring for 9 minutes. Meanwhile, remove peas from freezer.

Scatter peas over top of rice in 1 layer. Then top with cabbage and carrots. Do not mix. Cover and simmer 10 minutes or until rice is tender, liquid is absorbed, and peas are hot. Fluff rice gently with a fork. Taste and adjust seasoning. Serve topped with cilantro sprigs or leaves.

Makes 4 servings.

Mango Milkshake

1 (16-ounce) package frozen unsweetened mango, thawed
  but still cold
1 cup plain nonfat yogurt
1 cup nonfat milk
4 tablespoons sugar
1 cup cold water

In blender, puree mango with yogurt, milk, sugar and water until smooth. Serve in glasses.

Makes 4 servings.

Vegetable Burrito Brunch

• *Jicama and carrots with lemon juice and cayenne* •
• *Spicy bean burritos* •
• *Fresh avocado salsa* •
• *Papaya fruit salad* •

AMOUNT OF CALORIES FROM FAT: **24%**

Burritos are fun to eat and are great entrées for quick vegetarian meals. Basically, you prepare a tasty vegetable mixture and roll it up in a hot tortilla. I like a hearty filling of pinto beans, sautéed onions, roasted peppers, and tomatoes, but you can make numerous variations. I've had burritos with black beans combined with sautéed red onions, green peppers, and lightly cooked carrot strips, broccoli, and cauliflower. You can also serve the tortillas and vegetable medley on separate plates, and each person fills and rolls up his or her own tortillas. Avocado salsa makes a good substitute for guacamole, so you can enjoy the taste of avocado without eating a large amount of this oil-rich fruit. Be sure to also have a bottle of your favorite hot sauce on the table. This is a dairy-free menu, but if you like you can top each burrito with a dollop of nonfat sour cream. For dessert, serve a refreshing salad of papaya or mango mixed with bananas or blueberries modeled on the papaya and banana salad on page 118.

ALTERNATIVES:

⇨ Make the burritos with whole wheat tortillas.
⇨ Instead of using roasted peppers from a jar, sauté strips of red or green bell peppers with the onion.

GAME PLAN:

Step 1. Make burrito filling.
Step 2. Make carrot-jicama salad.
Step 3. Make salsa.
Step 4. Heat tortillas; fill burritos.

TIPS:

♥ Buy fat-free tortillas to make burritos and to accompany vegetable soups and stews.
☺ Use roasted peppers from a jar in vegetable fillings, stews, and salads.
☺ Use high heat when heating oil for sautéing, but make sure to watch the pan so the oil doesn't burn.

JICAMA AND CARROTS WITH LEMON JUICE AND CAYENNE

2 cups coarsely shredded, peeled jicama
2 cups shredded carrots
1 tablespoon olive oil
2 tablespoons strained fresh lemon juice
Salt and freshly ground pepper
Cayenne pepper
Pinch of sugar (optional)

Mix jicama, carrots, oil, and lemon juice. Season to taste with salt, pepper, and cayenne. Taste and add sugar if needed.

Makes 4 servings.

SPICY BEAN BURRITOS

1 tablespoon vegetable oil
1 large onion, halved and sliced
½ teaspoon hot red pepper flakes, or to taste
½ teaspoon dried oregano
1½ teaspoons ground cumin
1 (14½-ounce) can diced tomatoes
2 (15-ounce) cans pinto beans, drained
¾ cup diced roasted red bell peppers from a jar
Salt and freshly ground pepper
8 to 12 flour tortillas, preferably fat-free

Heat oil in a sauté pan, add onion, and sauté over medium heat 5 minutes or until beginning to turn golden. Stir in hot pepper flakes, oregano, cumin, and tomatoes and bring to a boil. Add beans and roasted peppers and heat through. Transfer about half the bean mixture to a bowl and mash it with a potato masher. Return mashed mixture to the pan and heat through. Season to taste with salt and pepper.

Layer a stack of 4 flour tortillas between 2 dampened paper towels and microwave on HIGH 45 seconds to heat through. Roll about ⅓ cup filling in each tortilla. Heat more tortillas and serve with remaining filling.

Makes 4 servings.

Fresh Avocado Salsa

1 fresh jalapeño pepper, quartered
½ cup packed cilantro sprigs
½ medium white onion, cut in 4 pieces
¾ pound ripe plum tomatoes, quartered
1 ripe medium avocado, preferably Haas
Salt

Wear gloves when handling hot pepper. Remove seeds if desired for less heat. Finely chop pepper and cilantro in food processor. Add onion and pulse on and off until onion is chopped. Add tomatoes to processor and pulse to coarsely chop. Peel and dice avocado and add to salsa. Mix well. Season to taste with salt. Serve at room temperature.

Makes 4 servings.

Falafel Burger Barbecue

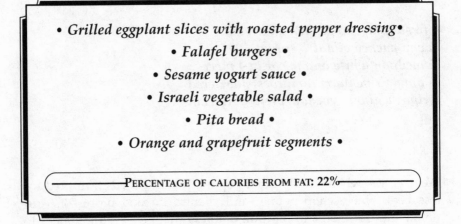

• *Grilled eggplant slices with roasted pepper dressing*•
• *Falafel burgers* •
• *Sesame yogurt sauce* •
• *Israeli vegetable salad* •
• *Pita bread* •
• *Orange and grapefruit segments* •

PERCENTAGE OF CALORIES FROM FAT: **22%**

Falafel can be a casual yet exotic party food. Traditionally, falafel balls are deep-fried, but in this new version I have greatly reduced the fat by shaping the falafel as burgers and grilling them. Made of chick-peas and flavored with onion, cumin, cilantro, and plenty of garlic, the grilled falafel are tasty and easy to prepare. Serve them on a plate or in a pita, with a salad of diced tomatoes, cucumbers, and shredded lettuce and sprinkle them with a little hot sauce, if you like. For an accompaniment, prepare a quick, low-fat sesame sauce instead of the usual tahini. As an appetizer or together with the falafel, serve grilled eggplant slices and top them with a vinaigrette enhanced with diced roasted red peppers.

ALTERNATIVES:

⇨ Falafel burgers make great vegetarian burgers and can be served the same way as meat burgers—on a hamburger bun, topped with tomato slices, red onion slices, lettuce leaves, pickles, ketchup, and mustard.
⇨ Instead of serving grilled eggplant as an appetizer, serve it with rice or bulgur wheat and a salad for a simple supper.

⇨ Add diced canned roasted chiles to the dressing for the eggplant slices instead of or in addition to the sweet peppers. Remember that these chiles are hot!
⇨ Serve grilled eggplant with fresh salsa instead of pepper dressing.
⇨ In Israeli salad, substitute shredded green or red cabbage for the lettuce.

GAME PLAN:

Step 1. Prepare burger mixture.
Step 2. Slice eggplant.
Step 3. Prepare salad.
Step 4. Prepare sauce.
Step 5. Prepare dressing for eggplant.
Step 6. Grill eggplant.
Step 7. Grill burgers.

TIPS:

♥ In many recipes that call for frying eggplant slices, you can prepare them in the broiler instead, as a tasty low-fat alternative.
☺ Leave peel on eggplant. If the eggplant's skin is smooth and shiny, it will not be tough or bitter.

GRILLED EGGPLANT SLICES WITH ROASTED PEPPER DRESSING

1 large eggplant (1¼ to 1½ pounds), cut into slices ½ inch thick
2 tablespoons olive oil
Salt and freshly ground pepper
2 teaspoons wine vinegar
¼ teaspoon dried oregano
⅓ cup diced roasted red bell pepper halves (from a jar)

Preheat grill and lightly oil it. Brush eggplant slices lightly with 1 tablespoon oil and sprinkle with salt and pepper. Grill slices over medium heat about 4 or 5 minute per side or until tender.

Meanwhile, whisk the remaining 1 tablespoon oil with vinegar, oregano, and salt and pepper to taste in a small bowl. Stir in diced roasted pepper.

Transfer grilled eggplant to a platter or to plates. Spoon dressing over eggplant. Serve hot, warm, or at room temperature.

Makes 4 servings.

FALAFEL BURGERS

6 large garlic cloves, peeled
¼ cup small cilantro sprigs
1 medium onion, peeled and quartered
2 (15- or 16-ounce) cans chickpeas (garbanzo beans), drained
2 teaspoons ground coriander
2 teaspoons ground cumin
½ teaspoon salt
½ teaspoon ground black pepper
2 tablespoons bread crumbs
1 egg white

Mince garlic and cilantro in food processor. Remove 1 teaspoon of mixture and reserve for Sesame Yogurt Sauce. Add onion to mixture in processor and mince it. Add chickpeas, coriander, cumin, salt, pepper, and bread crumbs and process with on-off pulses to a chunky puree, scraping down occasionally. Add egg white and process until blended. Transfer to a bowl. Mix well.

Shape mixture into 8 smooth patties. Pack mixture firmly when shaping so that burgers hold together.

Heat grill and oil grill bars. Grill burgers over medium heat about 5 minutes. Turn them over carefully with 2 spatulas and grill 5 more minutes or until slightly firm on top. Serve hot.

Makes 4 servings, 8 burgers.

SESAME YOGURT SAUCE

1 cup nonfat yogurt
1 teaspoon garlic-cilantro mixture (from Falafel Burger recipe,
  above)
1 teaspoon Asian sesame oil
Salt and freshly ground pepper

Mix yogurt, garlic mixture, and sesame oil in a bowl. Season to taste
with salt and pepper. Serve cool.

Makes 4 servings.

ISRAELI VEGETABLE SALAD

3 ripe medium tomatoes, cut into small dice
½ long (European) cucumber, cut into small dice
2 cups shredded lettuce (optional)
2 to 3 tablespoons chopped red onion or 1 green onion, sliced
1 tablespoon olive or vegetable oil
2 teaspoons strained fresh lemon juice
Salt and freshly ground pepper

Mix tomatoes, cucumber, lettuce, and onion in a bowl. Add oil, lemon
juice, and salt and pepper to taste. Serve cold or at room temperature.

Makes 4 servings.

CHAPTER 4

MENUS WITH RICE OR OTHER GRAINS

Lively Flavors for Winter

- *Carrot, cranberry, and water chestnut salad* •
- *Curried cabbage with rice* •
- *Beets with yogurt and dill* •
- *Pears in red wine with cinnamon* •

AMOUNT OF CALORIES FROM FAT: 9%

After shoveling snow or going for a brisk winter walk, you need something hot and satisfying. A plateful of golden curried cabbage with rice just fits the bill! But it does more for you. Cabbage is the best-known member of the cruciferous family of vegetables, which nutritionists believe help protect the body from cancer and so we should eat them several times a week.

Round out the menu with other winter produce items prepared with a delicious new twist. For an appetizer, try a crunchy salad of sweet ingredients—grated carrots, dried cranberries, and water chestnuts—complemented by a tangy citrus and ginger dressing. The dessert is an easy version of a classic loved in France and Italy. The pears' cinnamon-accented sauce reminds one of mulled wine and makes this dessert an ideal ending to a cold-weather meal.

ALTERNATIVES:

⇨ In the carrot salad, substitute thin strips of jicama for the water chestnuts.
⇨ Prepare the beet salad with fresh or dried mint instead of dill.

GAME PLAN:

Step 1. Prepare cabbage with rice.
Step 2. Prepare pears.
Step 3. Make carrot salad.
Step 4. Make beet salad.

TIPS:

♥ If nonfat yogurt is too tart for your taste, substitute nonfat sour cream in the beet salad.
♥ Salads made of sweet ingredients are good with tangy dressings composed of mainly citrus juice or vinegar and very little oil.
① Add vegetables when cooking rice to enhance the nutritive value of the entrée while saving on saucepans.
① Put cabbage half cut side down on a cutting board and shred it with a sharp, heavy knife.

CARROT, CRANBERRY, AND WATER CHESTNUT SALAD

1 (8-ounce) package shredded carrots (2¼ cups)
2 tablespoons strained fresh lemon juice
3 tablespoons orange juice
1 teaspoon vegetable oil
½ teaspoon ground ginger
Small pinches of salt and freshly ground pepper
¼ cup dried cranberries or raisins
1 (8-ounce) can sliced water chestnuts, drained

In a serving bowl, mix carrots with lemon juice, orange juice, oil, ginger, and salt and pepper to taste. Add cranberries and water chestnuts and stir to combine.

Makes 4 servings.

CURRIED CABBAGE WITH RICE

1 tablespoon vegetable oil
1 large onion, halved and sliced
1 small head cabbage (1 to 1¼ pounds), shredded, or 1 (1-pound)
   package shredded cabbage (7 or 8 cups)
1 teaspoon curry powder
Salt and freshly ground pepper
1½ cups long-grain rice
1 (14½-ounce) can vegetable broth (1¾ cups)

Heat oil in a large, wide casserole. Add onion and sauté over medium heat 3 minutes. Add cabbage and sprinkle with curry powder and salt and pepper to taste. Cover and cook over low heat 3 minutes; cabbage will wilt. Stir to combine vegetables with seasonings. Add rice, broth, and 1¼ cups hot water. Stir once and bring to a boil over high heat. Cover and cook over low heat without stirring for 17 minutes or until rice is tender. Taste and adjust seasoning.

Makes 4 servings.

BEETS WITH YOGURT AND DILL

2 cups plain nonfat yogurt
2 tablespoons snipped fresh dill, or 2 teaspoons dried dill
Salt and freshly ground pepper
1 (14- to 16-ounce) can sliced beets, drained

Mix yogurt with dill and salt and pepper to taste. Spoon into a shallow serving bowl. Fold beets partly into yogurt, so that yogurt remains white with some pink streaks and beets still show. Serve cold.

Makes 4 servings.

PEARS IN RED WINE WITH CINNAMON

1 cup dry red wine, such as Cabernet Sauvignon
⅓ cup sugar
½ teaspoon ground cinnamon
4 ripe medium pears (about 1½ pounds total)

Combine wine with sugar, cinnamon, and ½ cup water in a medium saucepan. Peel pears if desired. Halve pears and cut out their cores. Slice them crosswise into ⅜-inch-thick slices. Bring wine mixture to a simmer, stirring. Add pears and return to simmer. Cover and cook over low heat about 10 minutes or until pears are just tender. Leave pears in wine until ready to serve. Serve warm, at room temperature, or cold.

Makes 4 servings.

Dinner with Spanish Flair

• *Tomato salad with garlic and parsley* •

• *Vegetarian paella* •

• *Melon with strawberries* •

——— AMOUNT OF CALORIES FROM FAT: 13% ———

I have enjoyed paella in several regions of Spain, and what I loved best was the delicious rice. Olive oil, saffron, garlic, onions, tomatoes, and peppers make paella perfect for vegetarian cooking. After all, paella is basically rice cooked in a flavorful broth and dotted with lots of tasty ingredients. The rice in our paella gains a great taste from being cooked with the seasonings and aromatic vegetables. Peas and artichokes are traditional elements, but you can add other seasonal or frozen vegetables, such as diced zucchini, baby pattypan squash, corn kernels, or shredded carrots. And you don't need a special paella pan—a large skillet or sauté pan works fine. Paella is so satisfying that little else is required to complete the meal, so the menu is simple to prepare. A light salad before the entrée and perhaps a melon dessert or some guava, fresh figs, or other seasonal fruit are all you need.

ALTERNATIVES:

⇨ Instead of tomato salad, begin the meal with Mediterranean Diced Salad with Capers (page 35) or Baby Lettuce and Spinach Salad with Feta Cheese (page 88). Or follow the paella with a light green salad such as Butter Lettuce with Mustard Vinaigrette (page 45).

⇨ In the dessert, substitute blackberries for the strawberries.

GAME PLAN:

Step 1. Mince garlic for paella and for salad at same time;
         reserve 1 teaspoon for salad and use rest for paella.
Step 2. Prepare paella.
Step 3. Prepare dessert; refrigerate.
Step 4. Prepare salad.

TIPS:

♥ Vegetable broth adds a rich taste to rice dishes without contributing any fat.

☺ Buy diced melon at your market's salad bar to make preparing the dessert a snap.

☺ When small melons are available, buy 2 and serve ½ melon per person. This makes a pretty dessert and is faster because there's no need to peel and dice the melons. Just put the berries inside the melon halves and sprinkle them with the mixture of wine, sugar, and water.

TOMATO SALAD WITH GARLIC AND PARSLEY

1 teaspoon white wine vinegar
1 small garlic clove, minced (about ½ teaspoon)
1 tablespoon extra-virgin olive oil
Salt and freshly ground pepper
4 ripe medium tomatoes
1 to 2 tablespoons chopped Italian parsley

In a small bowl, whisk vinegar with garlic, oil, and salt and pepper to taste. Slice tomatoes and arrange slices slightly overlapping on a plate. Pour dressing evenly over them and sprinkle with salt, pepper, and parsley.

Makes 4 servings.

VEGETARIAN PAELLA

1 tablespoon olive oil
1 medium onion, diced
1 small red bell pepper, cut into strips about ¼ inch wide
1½ cups long-grain white rice
3 large garlic cloves, minced
1 (14½-ounce) can vegetable broth (1¾ cups)
¼ teaspoon saffron threads
1 (14½-ounce) can diced tomatoes, drained
Salt and freshly ground pepper
1½ cups frozen peas
8 ounces small mushrooms, halved
6 to 8 canned artichoke hearts (1 14-ounce can), drained, rinsed, and halved

Heat oil in a large skillet or sauté pan over medium heat. Add onion and bell pepper, and cook, stirring often, about 3 minutes or until softened. Add rice and sauté 1 minute. Stir in garlic, then add broth, 1¼ cups hot water, saffron, tomatoes, and salt and pepper to taste. Stir once and bring to a boil over high heat. Meanwhile, measure peas and let stand at room temperature. Cover rice and cook over low heat 7 minutes. Scatter peas, mushrooms, and artichokes over top of rice; do not stir. Cover and cook over low heat 12 minutes or until rice is tender. Let stand, covered, while you serve the first course of the menu.

Makes 4 servings.

MELON WITH STRAWBERRIES

½ honeydew melon (about 3 pounds)
3 tablespoons sugar, or more as needed
¼ cup dry red wine
1 (12-ounce) basket small strawberries, hulled

Cut melon into 1-inch dice; you will need about 6 cups. In a large bowl, mix sugar with wine and 2 tablespoons water. Add melon and strawberries. Mix gently; taste and add more sugar if needed. Refrigerate until ready to serve. Serve in dessert bowls.

Makes 4 servings.

Hearty and Healthful Supper

• *Bulgur wheat with kale, roasted peppers, and feta* •
• *Zucchini and corn medley with tomatoes* •
• *Sweet potatoes with mint-accented yogurt* •
• *Apples, oranges, or grapes* •

———————— AMOUNT OF CALORIES FROM FAT: **21%** ————————

This grain-based menu is tasty, is colorful, and features several nutritional powerhouses. Kale is a relatively neglected vegetable that deserves to appear on our plates more often—it's rich in nutrients like vitamins A, C, and E and contains iron and calcium as well. You also gain fiber from the bulgur wheat and calcium and protein from the feta cheese and from the yogurt topping on the sweet potatoes. Red peppers and sweet potatoes contribute generous amounts of vitamins A, B_6, and C. In addition to having all these dietary benefits, the meal is delicious and easy to prepare. A green salad topped with sliced, very fresh white mushrooms complements the menu well, either as a first course or following the main course.

ALTERNATIVES:

⇨ Instead of kale, you can use greens such as Swiss chard, mustard greens, or collard greens.

⇨ If you don't have bulgur wheat, you can prepare the entrée with quick-cooking brown rice or with couscous.

⇨ If you don't have roasted peppers, substitute fresh red bell peppers; add them to the bulgur wheat together with the broth.

⇨ Instead of zucchini, prepare a green bean and corn medley. Cook halved green beans about 6 minutes.

GAME PLAN:

Step 1. Prepare bulgur wheat recipe.
Step 2. Microwave sweet potatoes.
Step 3. For zucchini recipe, boil water while cutting zucchini.
    Cook zucchini and corn.
Step 4. Make yogurt sauce for sweet potatoes.
Step 5. Finish zucchini recipe.

TIPS:

♥ Feta cheese has less fat than grating cheeses. It's very flavorful, so a little goes a long way. Crumble it and sprinkle over grains or pasta.

☺ Warm vegetables are delicious with a cool, refreshing yogurt sauce made of nonfat yogurt with a few seasonings. Try the yogurt-mint sauce on steamed summer squash, microwaved winter squash, or cooked potatoes or carrots.

BULGUR WHEAT WITH KALE, ROASTED PEPPERS, AND FETA

1 bunch fresh green kale (12 ounces)
1⅔ cups medium bulgur wheat
2 large garlic cloves, chopped
1 (14½-ounce) can vegetable broth (1¾ cups)
½ teaspoon dried rosemary
⅔ cup diced roasted red bell peppers (from a jar)
Salt and freshly ground pepper
1 tablespoon capers, drained
½ cup crumbled feta cheese

Rinse kale and remove stems. Pile leaves and cut into thin strips about ½ inch wide.

In a heavy, large saucepan, dry-roast bulgur wheat with garlic over medium heat, stirring, 1½ minutes. Add broth, 1⅔ cups hot water, and rosemary. Stir and bring to a boil. Add kale and cover pan. Reduce heat to low and cook about 15 minutes or until water is absorbed and bulgur wheat is tender. Stir in roasted peppers. Season to taste with pepper; season lightly with salt if needed. Serve sprinkled with capers and feta.

Makes 4 servings.

ZUCCHINI AND CORN MEDLEY WITH TOMATOES

1¼ pounds small zucchini, cut into 1-inch dice
2 cups frozen corn kernels
2 teaspoons olive oil
1 (14½-ounce) can diced tomatoes, drained, or ¾ pound ripe
    tomatoes, diced
½ teaspoon dried oregano
Salt and freshly ground pepper

Add zucchini and corn to a saucepan of enough boiling water to cover them. Return to a boil over high heat. Cook 3 minutes or until zucchini is crisp-tender. Drain in a colander or strainer.

Heat oil in same saucepan, add tomatoes and oregano, and heat through over medium-high heat about 1 minute. Add zucchini and corn, sprinkle with salt and pepper to taste, and toss well. Serve hot.

Makes 4 servings.

SWEET POTATOES WITH MINT-ACCENTED YOGURT

4 medium orange-fleshed sweet potatoes or yams (about 2 pounds
 total)
1 cup plain nonfat yogurt
1½ teaspoons chopped fresh mint, or ½ teaspoon dried
Salt
Cayenne pepper

Pierce sweet potatoes with a fork in several places. Arrange them in a circle on a paper towel. Microwave uncovered on HIGH for 8 to 10 minutes, turning each potato over halfway through cooking; they should be tender when pierced with a fork. Wrap in paper towels until ready to serve.

Mix yogurt with mint and salt and cayenne pepper to taste. Serve cold or at room temperature, for spooning over halved sweet potatoes.

Makes 4 servings.

Supper for Any Season

• *Red and green cole slaw with pink grapefruit* •
• *Kasha with mushrooms and green onions* •
• *Lima beans with tomatoes and garlic* •
• *Pears or pineapple* •

—————— AMOUNT OF CALORIES FROM FAT: **26%** ——————

You can serve this menu at any time because it's based on ingredients from the pantry and on vegetables that are available year-round. The entrée is a quick, low-fat adaptation of a popular dish of kasha, or buckwheat groats. Kasha comes in three sizes—fine, medium, and coarse—and can often be found with the kosher products in your market. The first time you try it you might find its flavor unusual, but after you taste it a few times, you'll enjoy its earthy taste. If you like, embellish the kasha with a dollop of fat-free sour cream. With the kasha, serve a lively accompaniment of lima beans in a 2-minute tomato sauce. Begin the meal with a colorful cabbage and raisin salad topped with sections of pink grapefruit and dressed with raspberry vinegar.

ALTERNATIVES:

⇨ Substitute broccoli or canned lima beans or butter beans for the frozen lima beans. In spring, substitute asparagus for the lima beans; serve it in the same tomato-garlic sauce.
⇨ Cook 8 ounces bow-tie pasta or wide noodles and combine with the kasha-mushroom mixture.

GAME PLAN:

Step 1. Prepare kasha dish.
Step 2. Prepare lima beans.
Step 3. Prepare salad.

TIPS:

♥ Very little oil is needed to sauté garlic. Use just 1 or 2 teaspoons to sauté 2 to 4 chopped cloves. Sauté the garlic over low or medium-low heat only 10 to 20 seconds, so it doesn't burn.

☺ Buy packaged shredded red and green cabbage. It's much faster than shredding it with a knife!

☺ Kasha (buckwheat groats) is a fast-cooking grain—it takes only about 10 minutes to cook.

RED AND GREEN COLE SLAW WITH PINK GRAPEFRUIT

2 tablespoons raspberry vinegar
2 tablespoons vegetable oil
Salt and freshly ground pepper
3 cups shredded red cabbage
3 cups shredded green cabbage or cole slaw mix
¼ cup raisins
1 pink or red grapefruit

In a large bowl, whisk vinegar with oil and salt and pepper to taste. Add red and green cabbage and mix well to moisten cabbage evenly. Mix in raisins. Taste and adjust seasoning. Peel grapefruit and cut off most of white pith. Divide into sections. Mix half the sections gently with the salad. Top salad with remaining grapefruit sections.

Makes 4 servings.

KASHA WITH MUSHROOMS AND GREEN ONIONS

1 (14½-ounce) can vegetable broth (1¾ cups)
2 tablespoons vegetable oil
1 (6-ounce) package sliced mushrooms
Salt and freshly ground pepper
4 green onions, sliced
1 cup medium kasha (roasted buckwheat groats or kernels)
½ teaspoon dried tarragon

Pour broth into a glass measuring cup and microwave on HIGH until hot, about 2 minutes. Heat 1 tablespoon oil in a heavy sauté pan. Add mushrooms, sprinkle with salt and pepper and sauté, stirring, over medium-high heat 2 minutes. Add green onions and sauté ½ minute. Transfer to a bowl. Cover to keep warm.

Add remaining 1 tablespoon oil to the pan and heat. Add kasha and sauté over medium heat about 1 minute, stirring. Add hot broth, ¼ cup hot water, salt, pepper, and tarragon. Stir once and bring to a boil. Cover and cook over low heat 10 minutes or until kasha is just tender and all liquid is absorbed. Fluff with a fork. Use fork to stir mushroom mixture into kasha. Taste and adjust seasoning. Serve hot.

Makes 4 servings.

LIMA BEANS WITH TOMATOES AND GARLIC

1 (10-ounce) package frozen lima beans (2 cups)
1 teaspoon olive oil
2 large garlic cloves, minced
1 (14½-ounce) can diced tomatoes, drained
Salt and freshly ground pepper

Cook lima beans in a medium saucepan of boiling water 5 to 7 minutes or until tender. Drain. In same pan, heat oil over low heat, add garlic, and sauté 10 seconds. Add tomatoes and heat through. Add lima beans and season to taste with salt and pepper. Serve hot.

Makes 4 servings.

Speedy Weekday Menu

• *Brown rice with greens* •
• *Yellow squash in sweet-and-sour sauce* •
• *Strawberry-banana smoothie* •

AMOUNT OF CALORIES FROM FAT: 25%

Take advantage of a variety of fresh and packaged ingredients to make everyday suppers tasty as well as nutritious. In the frozen foods department, you can find many types of greens—not just spinach, but mustard greens, turnip greens, and collard greens. The main course here makes use of these greens along with quick-cooking brown rice, which is ready in 10 minutes. A light sprinkling of toasted nuts completes the dish. For a colorful accompaniment, serve yellow crookneck squash in an easy-to-make sweet-and-sour tomato sauce accented with raisins. You might also like to add a salad of cole slaw or broccoli slaw, such as Broccoli Slaw with Herb Dressing (page 48). Dessert couldn't be easier—a "fresh from the blender" drink that the whole family will love.

ALTERNATIVES:

⇨ Instead of mustard greens, prepare the rice with turnip greens or spinach.
⇨ Instead of nuts, you can sprinkle the rice with freshly grated Parmesan cheese; but be sure it's a *light* sprinkling.
⇨ If you don't have yellow crookneck squash, use zucchini or patty-pan squash.

GAME PLAN:

Step 1. Prepare rice.
Step 2. While rice cooks, prepare squash.
Step 3. Put banana and berries in blender. Prepare drink at
serving time.

TIPS:

♥ Use bananas and fat-free yogurt to make blender drinks thick and
luscious without adding fat.
☺ Buy ready-diced onion to save time chopping. You can find it in
the fresh or the frozen produce sections.

BROWN RICE WITH GREENS

2 tablespoons olive oil
2 large garlic cloves, chopped
1 (14½-ounce) can vegetable broth (1¾ cups)
1 (1-pound) package frozen chopped mustard greens
3 cups quick-cooking brown rice
Salt and freshly ground pepper
2 tablespoons coarsely chopped roasted almonds, pecans, or
  peanuts (optional)

Heat oil in a medium saucepan. Add garlic and sauté over medium heat, stirring, ½ minute. Add broth and ½ cup water and bring to a boil over high heat. Add greens, cover, and return to a boil. Simmer 3 minutes or until greens are separated. Add rice and mix well. Bring to a simmer. Reduce heat to low, cover tightly, and simmer, without stirring, 5 minutes. Remove from heat and let stand, covered, 5 minutes. Fluff rice gently with a fork. Season to taste with salt and pepper. Serve sprinkled with toasted nuts.

Makes 4 servings.

YELLOW SQUASH IN SWEET-AND-SOUR SAUCE

1 pound yellow crookneck squash
2 tablespoons vegetable oil
1 large onion, chopped
1 (14½-ounce) can diced tomatoes, drained
Salt and freshly ground pepper
¼ cup dark raisins
1 tablespoon strained fresh lemon juice, or more to taste
2 teaspoons sugar, or more to taste

Cut thin neck part of squash into ½-inch slices. Quarter thick part lengthwise and cut into ½-inch slices to form dice.

Heat oil in a large, heavy sauté pan, add onion, and sauté over medium heat about 5 minutes or until golden. Add tomatoes and cook uncovered 2 minutes. Add squash and salt and pepper to taste. Stir and bring to boil. Cover and cook over medium heat, stirring occasionally, 7 minutes or until squash is crisp-tender. Add raisins, lemon juice, and sugar and cook 1 minute. Serve hot.

Makes 4 servings.

STRAWBERRY-BANANA SMOOTHIE

1 ripe medium banana, sliced (about 1 cup)
1 cup strawberries, rinsed and hulled
1 cup nonfat milk
1 cup plain nonfat yogurt
2 tablespoons honey
¾ cup crushed ice

In a blender, combine banana, berries, and milk. Blend until smooth. Add yogurt, honey, and crushed ice. Blend briefly until frothy. Pour into glasses and serve.

Makes 4 servings.

CHAPTER 5

VEGETABLE
ONE-POT MENUS

Mediterranean Summer Brunch

- *Quick and slim ratatouille* -
- *Orzo with toasted almonds* -
- *Baby lettuce and spinach salad with feta cheese* -
- *Baguette or country French bread* -
- *Peaches or cantaloupe* -

AMOUNT OF CALORIES FROM FAT: **29%**

The nutritional benefits of the Mediterranean diet are now better known to us. This dining and cooking style utilizes plenty of vegetables and grains and little meat. Typical Mediterranean flavors, such as garlic, tomatoes, and herbs, provide a tasty way to enjoy food so that not much fat is needed. The preferred fat in the region, olive oil, is healthful when used in moderation.

Ratatouille, an aromatic vegetable stew with garlic and herbs, is one of the glories of Provençal cooking and is an outstanding example of this lively culinary approach. Naturally ratatouille is at its best in summer, when tomatoes, peppers, eggplant, and zucchini are at their peak. To save time, our speedy version makes use of Japanese eggplants, which are tender and cook quickly, as well as canned tomatoes.

Because the vegetables cook quickly, they retain their colors. Ratatouille is wonderful hot or cold as a vegetarian main course. In summer, conclude this meal with peaches, honeydew melon, or cantaloupe, either alone or as a refreshing dessert of Peaches with White Wine and Mint (page 101) or Melon with Strawberries (page 71).

ALTERNATIVES:

⇨ To make this a vegan menu, omit the feta cheese and top the salad with sliced fresh mushrooms or halved cherry tomatoes.

⇨ If you don't have Japanese eggplant, use a ¾-pound regular (Italian) eggplant. Cut it into ¾-inch dice.

⇨ For a heartier meal, you might like to add a warm hard-boiled egg to each plate.

GAME PLAN:

Step 1. Prepare orzo.
Step 2. While onion and peppers are sautéing, slice zucchini and eggplant and chop garlic.
Step 3. Cook ratatouille.
Step 4. While ratatouille is cooking, prepare salad.

TIPS:

♥ For best flavor with minimum fat, sauté vegetables briefly in just a little oil. Then add chopped tomatoes or liquid to finish cooking them.

♥ When buying toasted nuts, choose dry-roasted so that no oil is added.

① Instead of chopping basil leaves, serve sprigs of fresh basil so everyone can tear the leaves into his or her own ratatouille. Its impact will be even greater, and the guests will enjoy the aroma when they tear the leaves.

QUICK AND SLIM RATATOUILLE

2½ tablespoons olive oil
1 large onion, halved and thinly sliced
1 red and 1 green bell pepper, cut into ½-inch strips
¾ pound small zucchini, cut into ⅜-inch dice
Salt and freshly ground pepper
¾ pound Japanese eggplant, cut into ½-inch slices, or Italian
  eggplant, cut into ¾-inch dice
3 large garlic cloves, chopped
1 (28-ounce) can diced tomatoes, drained
1 teaspoon dried thyme
1 bay leaf
Fresh basil leaves or sprigs (for serving)

Heat 1½ tablespoons oil in a large, wide casserole. Add onion and peppers, and sauté 5 minutes over medium heat. Add zucchini and salt and pepper to taste. Cover and cook 3 minutes. Transfer vegetables to a bowl.

Heat remaining 1 tablespoon oil in the casserole. Add eggplant, salt, and pepper and sauté over medium heat, stirring, 2 minutes. Add garlic, tomatoes, thyme, and bay leaf and bring to a boil. Cover and cook over medium heat 5 minutes.

Return zucchini-pepper mixture to casserole of eggplant and mix gently. Bring to a boil. Cook uncovered over medium-high heat, stirring occasionally, 4 minutes or until vegetables are tender. Taste and adjust seasoning; season generously with pepper. Remove bay leaf. Serve hot or cold, garnished with fresh basil.

Makes 4 servings.

ORZO WITH TOASTED ALMONDS

1 teaspoon olive oil
1½ cups orzo or riso (rice-shaped pasta)
1 (14½-ounce) can vegetable broth (1¾ cups)
2 tablespoons dried onions
Salt and freshly ground pepper
¼ cup dry-roasted almonds

Heat oil in a heavy, medium saucepan. Add orzo and sauté over low heat, stirring, 1 minute. Add broth, 1¼ cups water, dried onions, and salt and pepper to taste. Stir and bring to a boil. Cover and cook over low heat 15 minutes or until orzo is just tender. Taste and adjust seasoning. Serve sprinkled with almonds.

Makes 4 servings.

BABY LETTUCE AND SPINACH SALAD WITH FETA CHEESE

3 cups mixed baby lettuces
3 cups spinach leaves, preferably baby spinach
1½ tablespoons extra-virgin olive oil
2 teaspoons red wine vinegar or lemon juice
Salt and freshly ground pepper
½ teaspoon dried oregano
¼ cup feta cheese, crumbled into bite-size chunks

In a shallow bowl, combine lettuces, spinach, olive oil, vinegar, salt and pepper to taste, and oregano. Toss well. Top with feta cheese.

Makes 4 servings.

A Taste of Asia

- *Vegetable soup with silver noodles, tofu, and cilantro* •
- *Mushrooms and baby corn with mint and hot peppers* •
- *Steamed jasmine rice* •
- *Green salad with water chestnuts and sesame dressing* •
- *Lychees, oranges, or kiwis* •

AMOUNT OF CALORIES FROM FAT: **14%**

Although this menu might appear exotic, most of the ingredients are available in good supermarkets. The Asian section at my local market carries many ingredients that are ideal for quick, low-fat vegetarian cooking. I go there to buy bean threads, jasmine rice, canned baby corn, straw mushrooms, and water chestnuts as well as sesame oil, rice vinegar, and naturally, several brands of soy sauce. Of course, you can find a greater variety in Asian specialty shops.

The main course is a super-fast stew seasoned with chiles and mint leaves. In this terrific Thai combination for flavoring vegetables, the mint's clean, fresh taste balances the heat of the peppers. The chiles are left in large pieces so they can flavor and garnish the dish, and can easily be removed by those who do not want to eat them. Before the entrée serve a light, easy vegetable soup containing bean threads, which are made from mung beans and resemble thin rice noodles when dry. Once they are cooked, the bean threads become transparent and so on Thai menus are often called silver noodles. Follow the meal with fresh lychees, or mix diced fresh pineapple with canned lychees. Another pretty and tasty combination is lychees, orange segments, and kiwis.

ALTERNATIVES:

➪ Flavor the vegetable stew with basil leaves instead of mint leaves.
➪ Add an 8-ounce can of straw mushrooms instead of or in addition to fresh mushrooms.
➪ If you don't have jasmine rice, use long-grain white rice. Steam it with only 3 cups water.

GAME PLAN:

Step 1. Prepare steamed rice.
Step 2. Cut vegetables for soup and for mushroom-corn sauté.
Step 3. Prepare mushroom-corn sauté.
Step 4. Prepare soup.
Step 5. Prepare salad.

TIPS:

♥ Asian sesame oil is great as a seasoning because you don't need much; a little of this distinctive oil goes a long way.
☉ When very thin bean threads are added to soups, they need only 2 minutes to cook.

VEGETABLE SOUP WITH SILVER NOODLES, TOFU, AND CILANTRO

2 (14½-ounce) cans vegetable broth (3½ cups total)
¼ teaspoon hot red pepper flakes
1 cup shredded carrots
2 cups shredded bok choy
1 (10½-ounce) cake firm light tofu, cut into ¾-inch cubes
1 (3½-ounce) package very thin bean threads
¼ cup cilantro leaves
Salt

Reserve ½ cup vegetable broth for mushroom and baby corn recipe (see below).

Bring remaining broth and 2 cups water to a simmer with hot pepper flakes in a medium saucepan. Add carrots, bok choy, tofu, and bean threads. Cook over low heat about 2 minutes or until bean threads are just translucent. Stir in cilantro. Taste and add salt if needed. Serve using tongs and a ladle.

Makes 4 servings.

Mushrooms and Baby Corn with Mint and Hot Peppers

1½ *tablespoons vegetable oil*
½ *pound medium mushrooms, halved*
2 *fresh red or green jalapeño peppers, halved lengthwise*
2 *large garlic cloves, minced*
½ *cup vegetable broth (reserved from vegetable soup recipe,*
   above)
1 *cup frozen peas*
2 *tablespoons soy sauce, or more if needed*
3 *(5½-ounce) cans baby corn, rinsed*
4 *green onions, cut into 3-inch pieces*
1 *cup whole fresh mint leaves*

Heat oil in a large skillet or wok over medium heat. Add mushrooms and hot peppers and sauté over medium heat, stirring, about 3 minutes or until mushrooms brown lightly. Stir in garlic, then add broth, peas, and soy sauce. Bring to a boil. Cover and simmer over medium heat for 3 minutes or until peas are tender. Add corn, green onions, and mint leaves and heat for 2 minutes. Taste, and add more soy sauce if needed. Let stand, covered, until ready to serve.

Makes 4 servings.

STEAMED JASMINE RICE

1½ cups jasmine rice
3¾ cups water
Pinch of salt (optional)

Combine rice and water in a large saucepan. Bring to a boil over high heat. Cover and cook over very low heat 15 minutes or until just tender. Let stand, covered, 5 minutes before serving.

Makes 4 servings.

GREEN SALAD WITH WATER CHESTNUTS AND SESAME DRESSING

2 teaspoons Asian sesame oil
1½ teaspoons rice vinegar
Salt and freshly ground pepper
2 cups romaine lettuce, torn into bite-size pieces
2 cups iceberg lettuce mix (lettuce, red cabbage, and carrot)
1 (8-ounce) can sliced water chestnuts, rinsed and drained
1 cup bean sprouts, rinsed

In a small bowl, whisk sesame oil with vinegar and salt and pepper to taste. Mix lettuces in a serving bowl, add dressing, and toss until greens are moistened. Add water chestnuts and bean sprouts and toss again. Taste and adjust seasoning.

Makes 4 servings.

Cool Weather Supper

• *Romaine and radish salad with oranges* •
• *Moroccan winter vegetable stew* •
• *Quick couscous with toasted pine nuts and currants* •
• *Pears or apples* •

—————— AMOUNT OF CALORIES FROM FAT: **21%** ——————

When we think of southern Mediterranean countries such as Morocco, images of summer food come to mind. But this region has also developed delicious vegetable dishes for cool weather, such as cabbage with hot peppers and cilantro; and potatoes and turnips cooked with garlic, parsley, and hot and sweet paprika. In this menu, carrots, potatoes, and broccoli simmer with sautéed onions, garlic, and cumin for a robust, flavorful entrée. When serving, spoon the vegetable's cooking liquid over the couscous as a sauce. You might also like to have a bottle of hot sauce on the table for adding to the stew or to its accompanying oil-free couscous. For dessert serve tasty winter pears or crunchy apples. Mint Tea (see page 35) is another pleasing finale for the meal.

ALTERNATIVES:

⇨ If your market carries winter squash cut into sticks or diced, you can substitute it for the carrots in the vegetable stew. Or add diced zucchini or crookneck squash for the last 10 minutes of the stew's cooking time.
⇨ Stir 2 or 3 tablespoons chopped cilantro into vegetable stew at the last minute.

GAME PLAN:

Step 1. Prepare stew; cut carrots and broccoli while potatoes are cooking.
Step 2. Prepare couscous.
Step 3. Prepare salad.

TIPS:

♥ To make the stew even leaner, substitute olive oil spray for the 2 tablespoons oil. Spray only enough to lightly moisten the bottom of the pan.

♥ Use vegetable broth to cook couscous, and it will taste good without any oil.

♥ To further lower the fat in the couscous recipe, omit the pine nuts.

☉ Use purchased diced onions, peeled garlic, and sliced carrots in the vegetable stew.

☉ Substitute frozen small potatoes for fresh ones in the vegetable stew and leave them whole.

ROMAINE AND RADISH SALAD WITH ORANGES

6 cups bite-size pieces romaine lettuce
6 small red radishes, sliced
1 tablespoon lemon juice
2 tablespoons vegetable oil
Salt and freshly ground pepper
1 large orange, peeled and cut into segments

Toss lettuce with radish slices, lemon juice, oil, and salt and pepper to taste in a bowl. Taste and adjust seasoning. Divide among plates. Top with orange segments.

Makes 4 servings.

MOROCCAN WINTER VEGETABLE STEW

2 tablespoons olive oil
1 large onion, diced
2 large garlic cloves, chopped
1½ pounds small red potatoes, quartered
4 large carrots, diagonally sliced ¼ inch thick (about 4 cups)
1 teaspoon paprika
1 teaspoon ground cumin
Salt and freshly ground pepper
¼ teaspoon hot red pepper flakes, or more to taste
2 cups small broccoli florets

Heat oil in a large, heavy sauté pan over medium heat. Add onion and sauté over medium heat 2 minutes. Stir in garlic. Add potatoes and 1½ cups hot water and bring to a boil. Cover and cook over medium-low heat 5 minutes. Add carrots, paprika, cumin, salt and pepper to taste, and hot pepper flakes. Bring to a boil. Cover and cook over medium-low heat 15 minutes, occasionally stirring gently. Add broccoli, cover, and cook 3 minutes or until vegetables are tender. Taste and adjust seasoning.

Makes 4 servings.

QUICK COUSCOUS WITH TOASTED PINE NUTS AND CURRANTS

¼ cup pine nuts or slivered almonds
1 (14½-ounce) can vegetable broth (1¾ cups)
1 (10-ounce) package couscous (1⅔ cups)
¼ cup currants or raisins

Preheat toaster oven or oven to 350°F. Toast pine nuts about 3 minutes or until lightly browned. Transfer to a plate.

Bring broth and ½ cup water to a boil in a small saucepan. Stir in couscous and currants. Cover pan. Remove from heat and let stand 5 minutes. Taste and adjust seasoning. Serve sprinkled with pine nuts.

Makes 4 servings.

Country Fare from Europe

• *Cucumber-pepper salad with walnut oil vinaigrette* •
• *Vegetarian cassoulet* •
• *Crusty French bread* •
• *Peaches with white wine and mint* •

—————— AMOUNT OF CALORIES FROM FAT: 17% ——————

Cassoulet, a flavorful bean casserole, is a symbol of French regional cooking. This robust dish of peasant origin has survived the numerous cooking trends and is a favorite for both eating at home and dining out. Like many country classics, cassoulet developed out of the need to use the products at hand. Recipes vary from one village to the next and from one cook to another. Some cooks like a prominent tomato flavor while others don't add any tomato. Some prefer cassoulet to be very moist and almost soupy; others want theirs relatively dry. Cassoulet is a perfect dish for adapting to fast vegetarian cooking. Instead of meat, I add shiitake and white mushrooms, which give the cassoulet a meaty texture. Flavored with garlic, tomatoes, onions, and herbs, vegetable cassoulet is hearty and rich-tasting. It needs only very simple accompaniments, like a colorful salad of cucumbers and red or yellow bell peppers or a green salad. To conclude the meal, set out a bowl of seasonal fruit or serve a light dessert of peaches in Chardonnay wine with fresh mint.

ALTERNATIVES:

➪ Instead of adding frozen baby onions to cassoulet, slice 1 large onion and sauté it before adding the garlic.

➪ If you have fresh basil, garnish each plate of cassoulet with a sprig or two.

➪ Serve Pears in Red Wine with Cinnamon (page 67) instead of peaches for dessert.

GAME PLAN:

Step 1. Soak shiitake mushrooms; cut remaining ingredients.
Step 2. Cook cassoulet.
Step 3. Prepare dessert.
Step 4. Prepare salad.

TIPS:

♥ To make this low-fat dish as lean as possible, reduce the olive oil in the cassoulet to 2 teaspoons.

♥ Because cucumbers are naturally moist, cucumber salads need very little dressing.

① Use canned beans to make quick cassoulet and other bean casseroles.

① A fast way to cut a bell pepper is to set the pepper on its side on a board and cut off about ¼ of the pepper lengthwise, then to turn the pepper and continue cutting. There's no need to separately cut out the core and the seeds don't scatter.

CUCUMBER-PEPPER SALAD WITH WALNUT OIL VINAIGRETTE

1 large cucumber
1 large red bell pepper, cut into 2 x ¼-inch strips
1 tablespoon walnut oil
2 teaspoons tarragon vinegar or white wine vinegar
Salt and freshly ground pepper

Peel cucumber if desired. Halve cucumber and cut into thin slices. In a shallow serving bowl, mix cucumber slices with pepper strips. Add oil, vinegar, and salt and pepper to taste and mix well. Taste and adjust seasoning.

Makes 4 servings.

VEGETARIAN CASSOULET

1 ounce dried shiitake mushrooms
2 tablespoons olive oil
3 large garlic cloves, chopped
1 (14½-ounce) can diced tomatoes, drained
1 teaspoon dried thyme
2 teaspoons dried basil
1 bay leaf
1 (10-ounce) package frozen baby onions
1 pound white mushrooms, halved
Salt and freshly ground pepper
2 (15- or 16-ounce) cans great northern beans or other white
    beans, drained
¼ cup unseasoned bread crumbs

Put shiitake mushrooms in a bowl. Pour boiling water over them, adding enough to cover them. Push floating ones down. Let soak 5 minutes. Remove from water with a slotted spoon. Cut shiitake mushrooms into bite-size pieces, discarding stems.

Heat oil in a large, heavy casserole over medium heat. Stir in garlic and sauté 10 seconds. Add tomatoes and cook 1 minute over high heat. Add 2 tablespoons water, shiitake mushrooms, thyme, basil, and bay leaf. Stir and bring to a boil. Add baby onions, white mushrooms, and salt and pepper to taste. Stir and return to a boil. Cover and simmer over medium heat, stirring occasionally, for 10 minutes or until mushrooms are tender. Discard bay leaf. Gently mix in beans. Heat through over low heat. Taste and adjust seasoning.

Heat broiler. Spoon mixture into a 9- or 10-cup casserole. Sprinkle with bread crumbs. Broil about 1 minute or until bread crumbs brown; watch carefully so top does not burn. Serve from the baking dish.

Makes 4 servings.

PEACHES WITH WHITE WINE AND MINT

¾ *cup dry white wine, such as Chardonnay*
¾ *cup bottled peach nectar*
2 tablespoons sugar
2 tablespoons chopped fresh mint
4 large ripe peaches
Mint sprigs for garnish (optional)

Mix wine with peach nectar, sugar, mint, and ¼ cup water until sugar dissolves. Pour into a glass bowl. Slice peaches into wedges and add to wine mixture. Mix gently. Refrigerate until ready to serve. Serve cold, in glasses or dessert dishes. Garnish with mint sprigs.

Makes 4 servings.

Make-Ahead Supper

• *Three-bean salad with herb dressing* •
• *Quick low-fat eggplant in tomato sauce* •
• *Easy rice pilaf* •
• *Cherries, grapes, or apples* •

AMOUNT OF CALORIES FROM FAT: **20%**

This menu is not only quick, delicious, and low in fat, it is also super convenient. The entire supper can be prepared up to two days ahead. Cook the dishes when you have time and serve them at your leisure. Family members can help themselves, as the eggplant and the rice reheat beautifully in the microwave. Both the savory eggplant and the bean salad gain extra flavor by marinating in their sauces as they wait in the refrigerator. The colorful salad of lima beans, green beans, and red kidney beans with yellow peppers and herb dressing is satisfying enough to make a light lunch on its own. For a lovely presentation and extra nutrients, serve the salad on a bed of bite-size romaine lettuce or baby greens.

ALTERNATIVES:

⇨ In the bean salad, substitute chickpeas (garbanzo beans) for the red kidney beans.
⇨ For a simple supper, serve the eggplant with flat Iranian bread or pita bread instead of rice, a small amount of Syrian cheese or feta cheese, and a green salad.
⇨ If you have fresh basil, you can use small sprigs of it to garnish the eggplant.

GAME PLAN:

Step 1. Begin rice pilaf.
Step 2. For eggplant dish, sauté onion and cook eggplant.
Step 3. Boil water for beans.
Step 4. Add tomatoes to eggplant.
Step 5. Cook beans.
Step 6. Finish bean salad.

TIPS:

♥ For a fat-free rice dish, prepare aromatic steamed rice. Follow the instructions for pilaf, omitting the oil and the step of sautéing rice. Use water from the cold water tap instead of hot water.
☉ Choose Italian-style canned stewed tomatoes seasoned with basil, garlic, and oregano to add extra flavor to vegetable dishes. They save time because they already include the seasonings.
☉ Use dried onions to flavor rice instead of taking the time to chop onions.

THREE-BEAN SALAD WITH HERB DRESSING

1 (10-ounce) package frozen lima beans
8 ounces green beans, ends removed, cut in half
½ red onion
1 (15-ounce) can red kidney beans, drained
1 yellow bell pepper, cut into thin strips
2 tablespoons extra-virgin olive oil
1 tablespoon herb vinegar
½ teaspoon dried thyme
Salt and freshly ground pepper

Add lima beans to a medium saucepan of boiling salted water, cover, and bring to a boil. Cook 5 minutes. Add green beans and return to a boil. Cook uncovered over high heat about 5 minutes or until both types of beans are tender. Drain, rinse with cold water, and drain well.

Cut the onion half into thin slices and separate them into half rings. In a bowl, combine cooked beans with kidney beans, onion, and bell pepper. Add oil, vinegar, thyme, and salt and pepper to taste and mix well. Serve cold or at room temperature.

Makes 4 servings.

QUICK LOW-FAT EGGPLANT IN TOMATO SAUCE

1½ tablespoons olive oil
1 medium onion, chopped
1¾ pounds Japanese or Italian eggplants, unpeeled, cut into
    1-inch dice
Salt and freshly ground pepper
1 (14½-ounce) can stewed tomatoes, preferably Italian style
    (with basil, garlic, oregano), with juice
1 teaspoon dried basil

In a large, heavy sauté pan or wide casserole, heat oil, add onion, and sauté over medium heat 2 minutes. Add diced eggplant, sprinkle with salt, and stir over heat until eggplant is coated with onion mixture. Cover and cook 5 minutes, stirring once or twice.

Stir in tomatoes and bring to a boil. Cover and cook over medium-low heat, stirring occasionally, 15 minutes or until eggplant is tender. Stir in basil and cook 30 seconds. Season to taste with pepper. Serve hot or cold.

Makes 4 servings.

EASY RICE PILAF

2 teaspoons vegetable oil
1½ cups long-grain white rice
3 cups hot water
3 tablespoons dried minced onion
1 bay leaf
Salt and freshly ground pepper

Heat oil in a large, heavy saucepan over medium heat. Add rice and sauté, stirring, 2 minutes. Pour hot water over rice, add onion and bay leaf, and stir once. Add salt and pepper to taste. Bring to a boil over high heat. Reduce heat to low, cover tightly, and simmer, without stirring, 15 minutes or until tender. Fluff rice with a fork and remove bay leaf. Taste and adjust seasoning.

Makes 4 servings.

CHAPTER 6

SOUP MENUS

Soup and Sandwich Lunch

• *Quick and velvety carrot soup* •

• *Bagel with light cream cheese, red onion, and roasted peppers* •

• *Romaine salad with toasted walnuts* •

• *Oranges or tangerines* •

AMOUNT OF CALORIES FROM FAT: **24%**

The popular American pair, soup and a sandwich, makes a nutritious, satisfying, low-fat lunch or supper and can be quick and easy besides. The secret to the soup's smooth, rich texture is a puree of carrots and rice. To prepare the soup, all you do is cook carrots with dried onion, thyme, bay leaf, rice, and vegetable broth, then puree the soup. Enrich the soup with a little milk and embellish each bowl of the creamy, pale orange soup with a sprinkling of chives. The sandwich is a vegetarian take-off on bagels with lox and cream cheese, with roasted red peppers substituting for the lox. Make the sandwich with fresh or lightly toasted bagels. Round out the meal with a simple green salad with a dressing of walnut oil and wine vinegar.

ALTERNATIVES:

⇨ Vary the taste of the bagel—use onion, sesame, poppy seed, whole wheat or any other flavor bagel that you like.
⇨ Instead of chives, garnish soup with chopped green onion or parsley.

GAME PLAN:

Step 1. Make soup.
Step 2. Toast walnuts for salad; prepare dressing.
Step 3. Finish soup.
Step 4. Finish salad.
Step 5. Prepare sandwiches at the table.

TIPS:

♥ Puree root vegetables like carrots along with a little rice to thicken soups and give them a creamy texture without any cream.
♥ Walnut oil is high in polyunsaturated fats and low in saturated ones. Hazelnut oil is similar to olive oil in its nutrients, being high in monosaturated fat and a good source of vitamin E. Use these oils to add a distinctive taste to salads, but remember that all oils are high in fat and should be used in small amounts.
① Buy toasted nuts from the snack portion of the market.
① If you wish to toast nuts at home, use a toaster oven; it heats much faster than a regular oven.
① When making a small amount of vinaigrette for a generous quantity of greens, whisk the vinaigrette ingredients in a small bowl and then mix them with the greens; the dressing will coat the greens more evenly.

QUICK AND VELVETY CARROT SOUP

1 pound carrots, scraped
1 (14½-ounce) can vegetable broth (1¾ cups)
2 tablespoons uncooked white rice
2 tablespoons dried minced onion
Salt and freshly ground pepper
½ teaspoon dried thyme
1 bay leaf
½ teaspoon sugar
1½ cups nonfat milk
1 tablespoon thinly sliced or snipped chives

Quarter carrots lengthwise, then cut into ½-inch pieces to make dice. In a heavy medium saucepan, combine carrots, broth, ¼ cup water, rice, onion, salt, and pepper to taste, thyme, bay leaf, and sugar. Cover and bring to a boil. Simmer, covered, over low heat about 15 minutes or until carrots and rice are tender. Discard bay leaf.

With a slotted spoon, transfer carrots and rice to a blender or food processor, reserving cooking liquid. Puree mixture. With machine running, pour in cooking liquid. Puree until very smooth. Return to saucepan. Bring to a boil, stirring. Add milk and bring to a simmer, stirring. Do not boil. Taste and adjust seasoning. Ladle hot soup into heated bowls and garnish with chives.

Makes 4 servings.

Bagel with Light Cream Cheese, Red Onion, and Roasted Peppers

4 bagels
4 tablespoons spreadable nonfat cream cheese
2 thin slices red onion, separated in rings
4 roasted red pepper halves (from a jar)

For each sandwich, split bagel. Lightly toast the bagel halves if you wish. Spread each half lightly with ½ tablespoon cream cheese. Top bottom bagel half with 1 or 2 red onion rings and a roasted pepper half. Set other bagel half on top.

Makes 4 servings.

Romaine Salad with Toasted Walnuts

¼ cup diced walnuts
2 tablespoons walnut oil
1 tablespoon red or white wine vinegar
Salt and freshly ground pepper
5 cups bite-size pieces romaine lettuce, or a 10-ounce package

Preheat toaster oven or oven to 350°F. Toast walnuts in oven about 3 minutes or until aromatic and very lightly browned. Transfer to plate.
In a small bowl, whisk oil, vinegar, and salt and pepper to taste. In a serving bowl, toss lettuce with dressing. Taste and adjust seasoning. Serve salad topped with walnuts.

Makes 4 servings.

Autumn Soup and Salad Dinner

• *Red salad* •
• *Zucchini salad with dill and green onions* •
• *Fat-free double mushroom-barley soup* •
• *Country bread—fresh, dry, or toasted* •
• *Pears or apples* •

AMOUNT OF CALORIES FROM FAT: 25%

For this easy menu, serve a colorful appetizer plate of two light salads side by side—one red and one green, followed by a hearty, satisfying soup. The red salad is a mixture of tomatoes and sweet red peppers dressed with olive oil, balsamic vinegar, and a sprinkling of thyme. For the green salad, you quickly grate the zucchini in the food processor before mixing it with oil, lemon juice, dill, and green onions. Ten-minute barley enables you to prepare a European classic, mushroom-barley soup, as part of a 30-minute meal. You'll probably need to visit a health food store to find the quick barley, but you can substitute 1¼ cups quick-cooking brown rice, which is available at the supermarket.

ALTERNATIVES:

➪ Serve the soup with toasted English muffins; if you like, spread them with a thin layer of peanut butter.

➪ To make the menu more hearty, you can add a hard-boiled egg to each appetizer plate.

➪ If you wish to include dairy products, you can embellish each portion of soup with a dollop of nonfat sour cream and a sprinkling of chopped fresh parsley or dill.

GAME PLAN:

Step 1. Prepare soup.
Step 2. Prepare zucchini salad.
Step 3. Prepare red salad.

TIPS:

♥ There's no need to sauté vegetables to have tasty soup. Simmer them in vegetable broth for good flavor.
☉ If you use boiling water, you can soak dried mushrooms for only 5 minutes instead of the usual 20 or 30 minutes.

RED SALAD

1 large or 2 medium red bell peppers, diced
4 large plum tomatoes, diced
1 tablespoon extra-virgin olive oil
½ tablespoon balsamic vinegar
½ teaspoon dried thyme
Salt and freshly ground pepper

Mix pepper and tomatoes in a serving bowl. Add oil, vinegar, thyme, and salt and pepper to taste. Serve cold or at room temperature.

Makes 4 servings.

ZUCCHINI SALAD
WITH DILL
AND GREEN ONIONS

1 pound small zucchini, unpeeled, coarsely grated
2 green onions, cut into thin slices
1 tablespoon snipped or minced fresh dill, or 1 teaspoon dried
2 tablespoons vegetable oil
2 to 3 teaspoons fresh lemon juice
Salt and freshly ground pepper

In a shallow serving bowl, mix zucchini with green onions and dill.
Add oil, lemon juice, and salt and pepper to taste and mix lightly.
Taste and adjust seasoning. Serve cold or at room temperature.

Makes 4 servings.

Fat-Free Double Mushroom-Barley Soup

1 ounce dried porcini, shiitake, or Polish mushrooms
3 medium carrots, diced
1 medium onion, diced, or ½ cup packaged diced
3 celery stalks, diced
2 (14½-ounce) cans vegetable broth (3½ cups)
½ cup quick-cooking barley
1 (6-ounce) package sliced mushrooms
1 teaspoon mild paprika
Salt and freshly ground pepper
Hot paprika or cayenne pepper

Pour enough boiling water over dried mushrooms to cover them. Let them soak for 5 minutes. Meanwhile, in a large saucepan, combine carrots, onion, celery, broth, and 2½ cups hot water. Cover and bring to boil. Cook, covered, over medium-low heat 3 minutes.

Remove soaked mushrooms, discarding liquid. Dice any large mushrooms. If using shiitake mushrooms, discard stems.

Add barley, fresh and dried mushrooms, mild paprika, and salt and pepper to taste to soup. Cover and simmer over medium-low heat 10 to 12 minutes or until vegetables and barley are tender. Add hot paprika to taste. Taste and adjust seasoning.

Makes 4 servings.

South of the Border Soup Supper

- *Tortilla soup with green chiles and tomatoes* •
- *Rice salad with peas and peppers* •
- *Papaya and banana with lime* •

——— AMOUNT OF CALORIES FROM FAT: 21% ———

Tortilla soup is a favorite throughout Mexico. In some homes it contains only tomatoes and onion. Other cooks might include zucchini or other squash, carrots, chiles, or sweet peppers. Adding chopped cilantro to the finished soup lends a fresh touch. In the classic version, fried tortilla strips are stirred into the soup. I use oil-free tortilla chips instead to lower the fat and save time. Many versions of this soup call for grated cheese, such as Monterey Jack, but I think the soup is lighter and tastier without it. Follow the soup with a pretty salad of white rice dotted with green peas, diced red peppers, and black olives, served on a bed of fresh romaine lettuce.

ALTERNATIVES:

➪ Substitute chickpeas for peas in the rice salad.
➪ Instead of adding fresh red peppers to the salad, dice 3 roasted red bell pepper halves from a jar and add them.

GAME PLAN:

Step 1. Cook rice for salad.
Step 2. Prepare soup.
Step 3. Finish rice salad.
Step 4. Prepare fruit salad.

☺ Use canned mild chiles to add flavor to soups and vegetable stews.
♥ Serve oil-free tortilla chips, potato chips, or fat-free crackers to accompany soups instead of croutons.

TORTILLA SOUP WITH GREEN CHILES AND TOMATOES

1 tablespoon vegetable oil
1 medium onion, chopped
2 large garlic cloves, chopped
1 (4-ounce) can diced mild green chiles, rinsed and drained
1 (28-ounce) can diced tomatoes, drained
1 (14½-ounce) can vegetable broth (1¾ cups)
3 medium zucchini or yellow crookneck squash, diced
¼ cup coarsely chopped cilantro
Salt
4 cups oil-free tortilla chips, crushed lightly

In a large saucepan, heat oil. Add onion and sauté over medium heat 3 minutes. Stir in garlic and chiles, then add tomatoes, broth, and 2 cups hot water. Cover and bring to a boil. Add zucchini and return to a boil. Simmer, covered, 5 minutes over medium-low heat. Add 1 tablespoon cilantro and salt to taste. Serve soup sprinkled with remaining cilantro and tortilla chips.

Makes 4 servings.

RICE SALAD WITH PEAS AND PEPPERS

1 cup long-grain white rice
Salt and freshly ground pepper
1½ cups frozen peas
1 large red bell pepper, diced
3 green onions, thinly sliced
¼ cup sliced black olives
1½ tablespoons white wine vinegar
2 tablespoons extra-virgin olive oil

In a large saucepan, combine rice and 3 cups water and add a pinch of salt. Bring to a boil. Meanwhile, measure peas and let stand at room temperature. Cover rice and cook over low heat 8 minutes. Add peas without stirring. Cover and cook 7 minutes or until rice is just tender but still firm; check by tasting. Transfer to a large bowl. Add red pepper, green onions, and olives; mix well.

Make dressing by combining vinegar, oil, and salt and pepper to taste in a small bowl; whisk to blend. Add to rice mixture; mix gently. Taste and adjust seasoning. Serve cool or at room temperature.

Makes 4 servings.

PAPAYA AND BANANA WITH LIME

1 medium papaya (about 12 ounces)
2 bananas
1 tablespoon lime juice
1 tablespoon sugar

Halve papaya, remove seeds, and remove flesh from skin with a spoon. Dice papaya. Slice bananas and mix with papaya. Add lime juice and sugar, and mix gently. Cover and refrigerate until ready to serve.

Makes 4 servings.

Comfort Food for a Cold Night

- *Red cabbage salad with apples* •
- *Super-quick vegetable pizza* •
- *Creamy winter squash soup* •
- *Warm pineapple with granola* •

───────── AMOUNT OF CALORIES FROM FAT: **26%** ─────────

Vegetable soups have long been family supper favorites in practically every cuisine. Their charm lies in their simplicity. You might think that homemade vegetable soups take a long time to prepare, but your soup can be ready in less than 30 minutes if you proceed efficiently. With only two or three vegetables, such as winter squashes, onions, potatoes, carrots, and turnips, you can create delicious hearty soups. Our soup has a delicate yellow hue and is flavored with onion, a bay leaf, and freshly grated nutmeg, which gives the soup a lovely aroma. Half the vegetables are pureed to thicken the broth to a lucious, creamy texture, while the rest are left in chunks to keep their identity.

Pizza is everyone's favorite fun food, and there's no need for it to involve lots of work or be high in fat. Just use a prepared crust, top it with fresh vegetables, and go easy on the cheese and oil. In our version the vegetables stay deliciously crunchy. If you would like a dessert, warm some diced pineapple, alone or mixed with sliced bananas, briefly in the microwave. Sprinkle the fruit lightly with granola and serve.

ALTERNATIVES:

⇨ For a spicy accent, add a sprinkling of hot sauce to the finished soup.

⇨ Top each serving of soup with a spoonful of fat-free sour cream and sprinkle it with chopped fresh dill, chives, or parsley.

⇨ Top pizza with roasted pepper strips instead of sliced peppers.

GAME PLAN:

Step 1. Preheat oven.
Step 2. Make soup.
Step 3. Make pizza.
Step 4. Make salad.

TIPS:

♥ For lower-fat pizzas, used split pita breads instead of Italian bread shells.

☺ Buy winter squash in its fastest-cooking forms—either halved and seeded, or peeled and cut into sticks.

CREAMY WINTER SQUASH SOUP

1 (1½-pound) piece of winter squash, such as banana squash or
  butternut squash
1 large baking potato (about 10 ounces)
1 large onion, chopped
1 (14½-ounce) can vegetable broth (1¾ cups)
1 bay leaf
Salt and freshly ground pepper
1 cup nonfat or low-fat milk
Freshly grated nutmeg to taste

Cut off squash peel. Remove any seeds or stringy flesh. Cut squash
into 1-inch cubes. Scrub potato and cut into ¾-inch cubes. In a large
saucepan, combine squash, potato, onion, broth, bay leaf, and salt and
pepper to taste. Cover and bring to a boil. Cook, covered, over medium heat about 15 minutes or until vegetables are tender.

Discard bay leaf. Ladle 2 cups of the vegetables and ¾ cup of the
broth into a blender. Puree mixture and return it to remaining soup.
Stir gently. Bring soup to a simmer. Stir in milk and heat through over
low heat; do not boil. Add nutmeg; taste and adjust seasoning.

Makes 4 servings.

SUPER-QUICK VEGETABLE PIZZA

4 individual ready-to-eat pizza crusts (Italian bread shells)
6 ripe medium plum tomatoes, cut into thin rounds
1 teaspoon dried oregano
2 red or green bell peppers, cut into thin slices
1 cup sliced mushrooms
Salt and freshly ground pepper
4 teaspoons extra-virgin olive oil
4 teaspoons grated Parmesan cheese

Preheat oven to 450°F. Set pizza crusts on a baking sheet. Put tomato slices on each pizza shell and sprinkle with oregano. Scatter pepper slices and mushrooms on top and sprinkle with salt and pepper to taste. Sprinkle evenly with olive oil, then with Parmesan. Bake 8 minutes. Serve hot.

Makes 4 servings.

Red Cabbage Salad
with Apples

2 tablespoons tarragon vinegar or red wine vinegar
2 tablespoons vegetable oil
1 teaspoon sugar
Salt and freshly ground pepper
1 (8-ounce) package shredded red cabbage (about 4 cups)
1 large apple (tart or sweet)

In a large bowl, whisk vinegar with oil, sugar, and salt and pepper to taste. Add red cabbage and mix well, until cabbage is evenly moistened. Peel apple and cut into ½-inch dice. Add to salad and toss. Taste and adjust seasoning.

Makes 4 servings.

Soup and Sandwich, Italian Style

• *Bruschetta* •

• *Tuscan bean soup with pasta* •

• *Italian sesame bread* •

• *Pink grapefruit with mint* •

AMOUNT OF CALORIES FROM FAT: **16%**

Perhaps one of the reasons for the popularity of *cucina italiana* is that even in restaurants, the food has the warmth of home cooking. Bruschetta, a favorite appetizer in Italian restaurants, could be described as a fancy version of tomatoes on toast. It is easy to make at home, from toasted Italian bread rubbed with garlic and topped with diced tomatoes, fresh basil, and olive oil. Follow it with a thick, hearty soup of white beans and pasta shells redolent of garlic, herbs, and aromatic vegetables. If you want a simple green salad with this menu, prepare Romaine Salad with Toasted Walnuts (page 110). You might like to serve the refreshing grapefruit dessert with a few Italian amaretti cookies.

ALTERNATIVES:

➪ Add any of these vegetables to the soup at the same time as the broth: 1 or 2 diced zucchini, ½ cup spinach leaves, 2 or 3 Swiss chard leaves cut into strips, or ½ cup frozen corn or green beans.

➪ Sprinkle chopped fresh Italian parsley on each bowl of finished soup.

➪ Vary the pasta shapes in the soup—bow-ties, stars, squares, wheels, or elbow macaroni are all good.

➪ Instead of the dessert, in summer you might want to finish the meal with grapes or fresh figs.

GAME PLAN:

Step 1. Prepare soup.
Step 2. Prepare tomato mixture for bruschetta.
Step 3. Prepare dessert; refrigerate.
Step 4. Finish bruschetta.

TIPS

♥ Reach for the peppermill rather than the cheese bowl to add zip to vegetable-pasta soups.
♥ Use the garlic-rubbed toast from the bruschetta recipe as a lean version of garlic bread to accompany pasta or salad suppers.
① Use olive oil spray to moisten the toast instead of brushing the oil on.

BRUSCHETTA

4 ripe large plum tomatoes, diced
About 2 tablespoons extra-virgin olive oil
2 tablespoons fresh basil strips
Salt and freshly ground pepper
4 thick slices Italian or French bread
1 garlic clove, halved

In a medium bowl, mix tomatoes with 1 tablespoon olive oil and 1 tablespoon basil. Season to taste with salt and pepper.

Toast bread. Lightly brush bread with olive oil. Rub both sides of toast with cut garlic. Top toast with tomato mixture, including juices, and let stand 1 or 2 minutes to soften slightly. Sprinkle with remaining basil and serve.

Makes 4 servings.

Tuscan Bean Soup with Pasta

1 tablespoon olive oil
1 medium onion, diced (or ⅔ cup packaged diced)
2 celery stalks, diced
1 medium carrot, cut into ½-inch dice
1 (14½-ounce) can vegetable broth (1¾ cups)
2 large garlic cloves, minced
½ teaspoon dried rosemary
1 cup small pasta shells
1 (8-ounce) can tomato sauce
1 (15- or 16-ounce) can cannellini beans or other white beans
1 teaspoon dried sage or basil

Heat oil in a heavy, medium saucepan over medium heat. Add onion, celery, and carrot and sauté, stirring occasionally, 3 minutes. Add broth and 2¼ cups water. Cover and bring to a boil. Cook over medium heat 5 minutes. Add garlic, rosemary, and pasta. Cook uncovered over medium-high heat, stirring occasionally, 5 to 8 minutes or until pasta is tender but firm to the bite. Stir in tomato sauce, beans, and sage and heat through. Taste and adjust seasoning. Serve hot.

Makes 4 servings.

PINK GRAPEFRUIT WITH MINT

2 grapefruit, preferably pink or red
6 tablespoons grapefruit juice
3 tablespoons sugar
2 tablespoons chopped fresh mint

Cut peel from grapefruit, removing most of the white pith. Separate grapefruit into segments. Mix grapefruit juice, sugar, and mint in a medium bowl. Add grapefruit segments. Refrigerate until ready to serve. Serve in dessert dishes or fruit cups, with the syrup.

Makes 4 servings.

CHAPTER 7

SALAD MENUS

A Salad Supper with Chinese Flavors

• *Rice noodle salad with peanut dressing* •
• *Tangy cucumber and red cabbage salad* •
• *Asian pears with pineapple and raspberries* •

AMOUNT OF CALORIES FROM FAT: **21%**

Cold noodles with peanut sauce make a popular Chinese starter. To serve it as an entrée, try a new version made with rice noodles, shredded carrots, straw mushrooms, and green beans. The easy dressing is made in the food processor and flavored with garlic, fresh ginger, and sesame oil. Have bottles of soy sauce and hot sauce on the table in case anyone wants more. Accompany the noodles with a refreshing cucumber–red cabbage medley dressed with rice vinegar and a touch of sugar. Pineapple juice makes a simple yet flavorful dressing for the fruit salad.

ALTERNATIVES

⇨ Add extra crunch by topping each portion of salad with about ¼ cup bean sprouts.

⇨ Substitute 1½ cups small broccoli florets or thin zucchini strips for the green beans.

⇨ Substitute regular pears or a 1-pound can of lychees for Asian pears; canned lychees are available in Asian markets and some supermarkets.

GAME PLAN

Step 1. Boil water to cook green beans and noodles.
Step 2. Prepare noodle salad.
Step 3. Prepare cucumber-cabbage salad.
Step 4. Prepare fruit salad.

TIPS:

♥ Rice noodles are fat-free and contain no eggs. And they need only a minute or two to cook.

① Cook green beans and noodles together to save time and water; to save even more time, use frozen green beans.

① Use packaged shredded carrots in the noodle salad and packaged red cabbage in the cucumber–red cabbage salad.

RICE NOODLE SALAD WITH PEANUT DRESSING

6 ounces green beans, ends removed, broken into three pieces
1 (9-ounce) package thin rice noodles or rice sticks (mai fun)
1 cup shredded carrot
1 (15-ounce) can straw mushrooms, drained
2 garlic cloves, peeled
1 (¼-inch-thick) slice fresh ginger, quartered
¼ cup smooth peanut butter
½ tablespoon rice vinegar
½ teaspoon sugar
2 teaspoons Asian sesame oil
2 tablespoons soy sauce

Add green beans to a large saucepan of boiling salted water and cook uncovered over high heat about 4 minutes. Add rice noodles and cook 1½ minutes, lifting noodles with tongs to separate them as they cook, or until noodles and beans are just tender. Drain in strainer, rinse with cold water, and drain well. Transfer to a large bowl. Add carrot and mushrooms.

Finely chop garlic and ginger in food processor. Add peanut butter, rice vinegar, sugar, ¼ cup warm water, 1 teaspoon sesame oil, and 1 tablespoon soy sauce. Process until well blended. Toss noodle mixture with remaining 1 teaspoon sesame oil, remaining 1 tablespoon soy sauce, and another ¼ cup warm water. Top with peanut dressing and toss to combine.

Makes 4 servings.

TANGY CUCUMBER AND RED CABBAGE SALAD

2 *medium cucumbers*
2 *tablespoons rice vinegar*
1 *teaspoon sugar*
1 *tablespoon soy sauce*
1 *teaspoon vegetable oil*
2½ *cups shredded red cabbage*
Freshly ground pepper

Cut cucumbers into thin slices. Whisk vinegar and sugar in a small bowl until sugar dissolves. Whisk in soy sauce and oil. In a salad bowl, toss cucumbers and red cabbage with dressing. Season to taste with pepper.

Makes 4 servings.

ASIAN PEARS WITH PINEAPPLE AND RASPBERRIES

2 *cups diced fresh pineapple (12-ounce package)*
1 *tablespoon sugar*
1 *Asian pear, diced*
1 *(6-ounce) basket raspberries (about 1⅓ cups)*

Reserve 2 tablespoons juice from pineapple and mix it with sugar in a small cup. Mix pineapple and Asian pear in a glass bowl. Pour dressing over fruit and mix gently. Add raspberries and toss lightly. Serve cold.

Makes 4 servings.

Summer Salad Buffet

• *Pasta shells with marinated artichokes and red peppers* •
• *Tricolor salad* •
• *Baguette or Italian bread* •
• *Peaches and cream shortcakes* •

AMOUNT OF CALORIES FROM FAT: **27%**

The only ingredient that needs cooking in this menu is the pasta. Yet this tasty meal is perfect for a family supper or a casual get-together with friends. As a main course, serve a zesty pasta salad flavored with a lemon-oregano dressing and accented with a few treats—black olives, roasted red peppers, and marinated artichokes. If you want to vary this salad, tomato pasta shells or spirals also give a pretty result. With the pasta serve a low-fat take-off of a favorite Italian appetizer salad of tomatoes, mozzarella cheese, and fresh basil leaves, in which fresh white mushrooms replace the cheese. Prepare a new version of a classic American dessert—an incredibly easy, low-fat peach short-cake. It's quickly made with shortcake dessert cups, which are individual sponge cake shells usually sold at the produce department. Fill the cups with luscious fresh peaches and low-fat vanilla cream and top each dessert with a ripe strawberry.

ALTERNATIVES:

➪ Serve the pasta on a bed of romaine lettuce.
➪ Garnish the pasta salad with 1 or 2 hard-boiled eggs, cut into quarters.
➪ For a simpler dessert, omit the shortcake cups; mix the sliced peaches with sliced strawberries and top them with the vanilla sour cream mixture.

GAME PLAN:

Step 1. Prepare pasta salad.
Step 2. Prepare tomato-mushroom salad.
Step 3. Prepare dessert.

TIPS:

♥ Create other desserts by topping sliced angel food cake with the nonfat sour cream and vanilla mixture, then with fresh fruit.
☉ Keep marinated, roasted, and pickled vegetables in your pantry to add flavor to pasta salads.

PASTA SHELLS WITH MARINATED ARTICHOKES AND RED PEPPERS

8 ounces medium pasta shells (about 3 cups)
1½ tablespoons lemon juice
3 tablespoons extra-virgin olive oil
½ teaspoon dried leaf oregano, crumbled
Cayenne pepper
Salt and freshly ground pepper
1 (6-ounce) jar or 1 cup drained marinated artichokes, cut into bite-size pieces
⅓ cup sliced black olives
⅔ cup roasted red bell pepper strips (from a jar)
2 green onions, sliced

Cook pasta uncovered in a large pot of boiling salted water over high heat, stirring occasionally, about 8 minutes or until tender but firm to the bite. Meanwhile, make dressing: whisk lemon juice in a large bowl with oil, oregano, and cayenne pepper, salt, and pepper to taste.

Drain pasta, rinse with cold water, and drain well. Add to bowl of dressing and mix. Add artichokes, olives, roasted peppers, and green onions and mix gently. Taste and adjust seasoning.

Makes 4 servings.

TRICOLOR SALAD

4 large plum tomatoes
8 large white mushrooms
4 teaspoons extra-virgin olive oil
Salt and freshly ground pepper
8 basil leaves, cut into thin strips

Halve tomatoes lengthwise and put them on a board, cut side down. Slice about ¼ inch thick, keeping the slices of each half together. Transfer the cut tomato halves to a platter or to plates. Cut off mushroom stems. Cut caps into slices about ¼ inch thick. Arrange mushroom slices between the tomato slices. Sprinkle with oil, then with salt, pepper, and basil strips.

Makes 4 servings.

PEACHES AND CREAM
SHORTCAKES

1 cup nonfat sour cream
2 tablespoons sugar
1 teaspoon vanilla extract
4 shortcake dessert cups
2 large ripe peaches
2 strawberries, halved lengthwise

Mix sour cream, 1 tablespoon sugar, and vanilla. Put each shortcake dessert cup on a dessert plate. Spoon ¼ cup of the sour cream mixture into each dessert cup. Cut peaches into thin slices. In a bowl, mix peach slices with remaining 1 tablespoon sugar. Set some peach slices on top of each shortcake cup and garnish with ½ strawberry. Arrange remaining peach slices on the plate.

Makes 4 servings.

Warm Weather Brunch

• *Brown rice tabbouleh* •
• *Carrots and corn with spiced yogurt* •
• *Easy melon soup* •

—————— AMOUNT OF CALORIES FROM FAT: 14% ——————

Nutritious whole grains can make lively entrées when enhanced with generous amounts of fresh vegetables and herbs.

For this Mediterranean brunch or summer supper, the main course is a tasty new version of tabbouleh, a Lebanese salad classically made with bulgur wheat, tomatoes, mint, and plenty of parsley. Since bulgur wheat is not always easy to find, I like to prepare a low-fat adaptation of the dish using quick-cooking brown rice. In color and taste, the result is similar to the bulgur wheat version. If you like, serve the tabbouleh over lettuce and garnish it with sweet cherry tomatoes. Accompany it with vegetables dressed with cumin- and cayenne-spiked yogurt. Finish the meal with a pastel orange cantaloupe soup, a refreshing dessert that is one of the simplest to make—you just puree the cantaloupe with citrus juices and sugar.

ALTERNATIVES:

⇨ Add 3 tablespoons Midori (melon liqueur) to the soup.
⇨ Garnish each bowl of cantaloupe soup with 5 or 6 cantaloupe or honeydew melon balls; you can often buy them in your supermarket's salad bar or frozen foods aisle.

GAME PLAN:

Step 1. Cook brown rice.
Step 2. Cook carrots and corn.
Step 3. Chop parsley and mint for brown rice salad in food processor; wipe processor.
Step 4. Prepare melon soup.
Step 5. Finish rice salad.
Step 6. Prepare yogurt sauce.

TIPS:

♥ Low-fat salads of brown or white rice taste best when freshly made and still slightly warm. If you prepare them ahead, they will seem dry when cold. Let these salads stand out of the refrigerator for 10 minutes or microwave them very briefly to take off the chill.

☺ Use a food processor to chop parsley and skip the tedious step of removing individual leaves from the small stems. The machine can chop small stems fine.

BROWN RICE TABBOULEH

3 cups quick-cooking brown rice
6 ripe plum tomatoes
½ regular cucumber or ⅓ long (European) cucumber, peeled if desired
2 cups small parsley sprigs, rinsed and patted dry
⅓ cup fresh mint leaves
2 tablespoons strained fresh lemon juice
2 tablespoons extra-virgin olive oil
Salt and freshly ground black pepper
3 green onions, thinly sliced

Cook rice according to package directions. Transfer it to a large bowl.

Dice tomatoes and cucumber small (about ½ inch). Chop parsley and mint leaves together in a food processor.

Add lemon juice, olive oil, and salt and pepper to taste to rice. Add tomatoes, cucumber, and green onions and toss. Lightly stir in parsley mixture. Taste and adjust seasoning. Serve at room temperature.

Makes 4 servings.

CARROTS AND CORN WITH SPICED YOGURT

4 medium carrots, scraped and sliced ¼ inch thick
1½ cups frozen corn kernels
1 cup nonfat yogurt
½ teaspoon ground cumin
Salt
Cayenne pepper

Put carrots in a saucepan and add hot water to cover. Bring to a boil. Cook over medium heat 7 minutes. Add corn, cover, and bring to a boil. Cook over medium heat 3 minutes more or until carrots and corn are tender.

Meanwhile, mix yogurt with cumin and salt and cayenne pepper to taste. Drain vegetables. Serve them warm or at room temperature, topped with spiced yogurt.

Makes 4 servings.

EASY MELON SOUP

1 large ripe cantaloupe (3¼ to 3½ pounds)
¼ cup strained fresh orange juice
2 tablespoons strained fresh lemon juice, or more to taste
3 tablespoons sugar, or more to taste

Halve cantaloupe, remove seeds, and cut peel from flesh. Cut cantaloupe into chunks; you will need 4½ to 5 cups. Put chunks in a blender or food processor. Add lemon juice, orange juice, and sugar and process until smooth. Add ¼ cup water and process until blended. Taste, and add more sugar or lemon juice if desired. Refrigerate until ready to serve. Stir before serving.

Makes 4 servings.

Easy Party Menu

- *Roasted pepper, fresh mozzarella, and watercress sandwich* •
- *Black bean salad with red onions, tomatoes, and garlic-cumin dressing* •
- *Rice salad with dried cranberries and walnuts* •
- *Seasonal fruit; or angel food cake with berries and low-fat vanilla ice cream* •

AMOUNT OF CALORIES FROM FAT: **24%**

By making use of prepared ingredients and with minimal cooking, you can have a tasty, low-fat party menu in a flash. An effortless and nutritious way to begin the meal is to serve a refreshing glass of tomato juice or top-quality carrot juice, garnished with a lemon slice on the edge of the glass. The Cuban-inspired black bean salad is delicious and aromatic with its spicy dressing. For a pretty presentation and extra nutrients, you can serve the bean salad on a bed of green leaf lettuce or romaine. It looks lovely and festive when accompanied by the colorful rice salad flavored with fresh mint and green onions. For an easy way to add a vegetable, simply open a bag of shredded carrots and add them to the rice for the last few minutes of its cooking time. If you'd like a dessert, fill the hollow center of a purchased angel food cake with sweetened fresh berries.

ALTERNATIVES:

▷ In the sandwich, substitute sliced goat cheese or Armenian string cheese for the mozzarella.

▷ In the rice salad, substitute raisins or currants for the dried cranberries.

GAME PLAN:

Step 1. Cook rice.
Step 2. Prepare bean salad.
Step 3. Prepare rice salad.
Step 4. Prepare sandwiches.

TIPS:

♥ Instead of spreading butter on bread for sandwiches, brush the bread very lightly with olive oil.
♥ For a lower-fat appetizer, spread the bread with fat-free cream cheese instead of olive oil and omit the mozzarella.
☉ Serve open-face sandwiches as quick appetizers. Other good ingredients for topping them are tomato slices, basil leaves, sliced marinated mushrooms, or lightly cooked tips of pencil-thin asparagus.

ROASTED PEPPER, FRESH MOZZARELLA, AND WATERCRESS SANDWICH

4 thin slices country bread (about 3 inches in diameter)
1½ teaspoons extra-virgin olive oil
¾ cup watercress sprigs, top leafy part only
2 roasted pepper halves (from a jar), each cut into 2 pieces
3 ounces fresh mozzarella cheese, cut into 4 slices

Lightly toast the bread. Brush toast lightly with olive oil. Top each piece with a few watercress sprigs and a roasted pepper piece, then with a mozzarella slice. Serve at room temperature.

Makes 4 servings.

BLACK BEAN SALAD WITH RED ONIONS, TOMATOES, AND GARLIC-CUMIN DRESSING

1 tablespoon lime juice
2 large garlic cloves, minced
1 teaspoon ground cumin
2 tablespoons extra-virgin olive oil
Salt and freshly ground pepper
Cayenne pepper
2 (15-ounce) cans black beans, drained
½ red onion, chopped
4 plum tomatoes, diced
3 tablespoons chopped cilantro or parsley (optional)

In a medium serving bowl, whisk lime juice with garlic, cumin, olive oil, and salt, pepper, and cayenne pepper to taste. Add beans and mix gently. Add onion, tomatoes, and cilantro and gently mix again. Taste and adjust seasoning.

Makes 4 servings.

RICE SALAD WITH DRIED CRANBERRIES AND WALNUTS

1½ cups long-grain white rice
Salt and freshly ground pepper
1½ cups shredded carrots
1 tablespoon herb or white wine vinegar
2 tablespoons vegetable oil
¼ cup dried cranberries
¼ cup diced walnuts
¼ cup chopped fresh mint

In a large saucepan, combine rice, 3 cups water, and a pinch of salt. Bring to a boil. Cover and cook over low heat 10 minutes. Sprinkle carrots over top, cover, and cook 5 minutes or until rice is tender; check by tasting. Transfer to a bowl. Add vinegar, oil, salt, and pepper and mix gently. Add cranberries and walnuts, and again mix gently. Add mint. Taste and adjust seasoning.

Makes 4 servings.

Festive Family Supper

- *Ravioli, tomato, and lima bean salad with pesto dressing* •
- *French corn salad with peppers* •
- *Blueberry-banana crunch* •

—————— AMOUNT OF CALORIES FROM FAT: 24% ——————

This is a menu that all members of the family will like, as it contains everybody's favorites—corn, ravioli, and a tempting dessert. The corn salad is inspired by a dish I enjoyed at *charcuteries* in Paris. The star attraction for me in these alluring food stores was always the house salads, because they gave me ideas for delicious dishes I could easily make at home. One of the most popular items of these French "delis" is a colorful salad of corn dotted with red and green peppers. It is very easy to prepare and makes an attractive buffet dish. You can even make it a day or two ahead. This simple salad is also a perfect dish to bring to picnics or potlucks because everybody loves it, even children. Along with it serve a hearty salad of cheese-filled ravioli, ripe tomatoes, and cooked vegetables moistened with a boldly flavored vinaigrette made of pesto and a touch of balsamic vinegar. Dessert is a refreshing salad of blueberries and bananas, topped with fat-free sour cream and sprinkled with granola.

ALTERNATIVES:

⇨ In the ravioli salad, substitute pattypan squash for the zucchini.
⇨ Add 2 sliced celery stalks to the corn salad.

GAME PLAN:

Step 1. Boil 2 pots water, for ravioli and for corn.
Step 2. Cut vegetables.
Step 3. Cook lima beans, pasta, and squash; continue cutting
vegetables.
Step 4. Cook corn.
Step 5. Finish salads.
Step 6. Make dessert.

TIPS:

♥ Choose reduced-fat ravioli.
♥ To make a 3-serving package of ravioli (9 ounces) enough to serve
4, mix it with beans.
☺ To make corn salad even more quickly, use drained canned corn
kernels.
☺ Use purchased pesto to perk up pasta and cooked vegetable salads.

RAVIOLI, TOMATO, AND LIMA BEAN SALAD WITH PESTO DRESSING

1 (10-ounce) package frozen lima beans
¼ cup prepared pesto
2 tablespoons extra-virgin olive oil
1 tablespoon balsamic vinegar
1 (9-ounce) package fresh light cheese ravioli
3 medium zucchini, diced
8 ounces ripe tomatoes, cut into ½-inch dice
Salt and freshly ground pepper

Add lima beans to a large saucepan of boiling water, return to a boil, and cook over medium heat 5 minutes. Meanwhile, in a large serving bowl, stir pesto with olive oil and vinegar.

Add ravioli to pan of lima beans and bring to a boil. Add zucchini and cook 4 minutes more or until ravioli and vegetables are tender. Drain and rinse with cold water. Drain well. Transfer pasta mixture to bowl of pesto dressing, add tomatoes, and toss gently. Season to taste with salt and pepper.

Makes 4 servings.

FRENCH CORN SALAD WITH PEPPERS

1 (1-pound) package frozen corn kernels
1 red bell pepper, finely diced
1 green bell pepper, finely diced
2 tablespoons vegetable or olive oil
2 teaspoons tarragon or white wine vinegar
Salt and freshly ground pepper
4 cups baby lettuce, "European" lettuce mix, or mesclun

Add corn to a medium saucepan of boiling water. Return to a boil and simmer uncovered over medium-high heat 2 minutes or until just tender. Rinse with cold water and drain well.

In a medium bowl, combine corn, red and green peppers, oil, vinegar, and salt and pepper to taste. Mix well; taste and adjust seasoning. Make a bed of lettuce on each plate. Serve salad on lettuce.

Makes 4 servings.

BLUEBERRY-BANANA CRUNCH

2 bananas
1 (1-pint) basket blueberries (2 cups)
1⅓ cups nonfat sour cream
1 teaspoon vanilla extract
¼ cup granola or granola-type cereal

Slice bananas and mix with blueberries. Divide among 4 dessert dishes. Mix sour cream and vanilla. Top each serving of fruit with about ⅓ cup sour cream mixture. Refrigerate until ready to serve. At serving time, sprinkle with granola.

Makes 4 servings.

CHAPTER 8

BONUS RECIPES

SAVORY RECIPES

QUICK AND LEAN HUMMUS

Hummus, or chickpea dip, is a favorite spread in the Middle East. It is accompanied most often by pita bread, but is also good with country-style bread. If you would like to follow tradition, serve the hummus sprinkled with parsley, paprika, or a little cayenne pepper.

2 large garlic cloves, peeled
2 (15- to 16-ounce) cans chickpeas, drained and rinsed
2 tablespoons strained fresh lemon juice
2 tablespoons extra-virgin olive oil
About ½ cup water
Salt
Cayenne pepper

Mince garlic in food processor. Add chickpeas and process to chop. Add lemon juice, oil, and ¼ cup water and puree until finely blended. Add more water if necessary so that mixture has consistency of a smooth spread. Season to taste with salt and cayenne. *Spread can be kept about 4 days in refrigerator.*

Makes 2½ cups, about 8 servings.

GRILLED EGGPLANT SPREAD WITH GARLIC

It's great to have a vegetable dip on hand for spreading on bread instead of using butter or margarine. This delectable Mediterranean appetizer is also known as eggplant caviar. Serve it with pita or Italian bread.

You can bake the eggplants in the oven or grill them in a broiler or on a grill. If you want to use the broiler, choose fairly slender eggplants so they will fit. Small, zucchini-size Japanese or Chinese eggplants are wonderful prepared this way too, and take only about one-third the time to cook as large eggplants do.

These are the easiest ways to cook eggplants, as they are cooked whole. Prepared this way, they can be virtually fat-free. Although their cooking time is not short, you can basically leave the eggplants unattended; all you need to do is turn them from time to time.

2 medium eggplants (about 2¼ pounds total)
1 medium garlic clove, finely minced
1 to 2 tablespoons extra-virgin olive oil
1 to 2 teaspoons strained fresh lemon juice
1 to 2 tablespoons chopped parsley or cilantro (optional)
Salt and freshly ground pepper

Prick eggplants a few times with a fork. Grill eggplants above medium-hot coals about 1 hour or broil about 40 minutes, turning often, until skin blackens, flesh is tender, and eggplants look collapsed.

If you prefer to bake the eggplant, preheat oven to 400°F. After piercing eggplants, bake them on a large foil-lined baking sheet for 30 minutes. Turn eggplants over and bake them 30 to 40 minutes or until very tender when pricked with a fork.

Leave eggplants until cool enough to handle. Remove eggplant skin and cut off caps. Halve eggplant and drain off any liquid inside. Use a food processor or knife to chop eggplant flesh to a chunky puree.

In a large bowl, combine eggplant, garlic, oil, lemon juice, parsley, and salt and pepper to taste and mix well. Mixture should be highly seasoned. Refrigerate at least 30 minutes before serving. *Spread can be kept about 4 days in refrigerator.*

Makes 4 or 5 servings.

MUSHROOM-TOMATO SAUCE

This is a basic sauce that is convenient to keep in the freezer for a tasty quick meal. Use the sauce as it is, or add chopped fresh tarragon or parsley. Serve it as a flavorful topping for pasta or grains.

1 tablespoon olive oil
2 tablespoons minced shallots
4 ounces mushrooms, halved and thinly sliced
Salt and freshly ground pepper
1 (28-ounce) and 1 (14½-ounce) can diced tomatoes, drained
½ teaspoon dried thyme
1 bay leaf
½ cup vegetable broth

Heat oil in a medium skillet. Add shallots, mushrooms, and salt and pepper to taste and sauté over medium-high heat about 3 minutes or until mushrooms are lightly browned. Transfer to a bowl. To skillet from cooking mushrooms, add tomatoes, thyme, bay leaf, salt, and pepper. Cook over medium heat, stirring often, 15 minutes or until sauce is thick. Discard bay leaf. Add broth and bring to a boil. Add mushroom mixture. Serve hot. *Sauce can be kept, covered, 2 days in refrigerator; or it can be frozen.*

Makes about 1¾ cups, about 4 servings.

SWEET RECIPES

THE PERFECT STRAWBERRY PIE

Strawberry pie made with truly ripe strawberries is one of the best treats of spring. This no-bake strawberry pie is ideal for today's cooks. It is delicious, beautiful, and has a creamy, fat-free vanilla filling. It's possibly the easiest strawberry pie ever. The trick is to use ready-to-eat packaged pie crust and terrific new dairy products—nonfat cream cheese and sour cream. You don't even need to cook the filling. All you do is spoon it into the crust and top it with fresh strawberries.

For a festive touch, coat the strawberries with a glaze made from red currant jelly, as they do in elegant French patisseries. Just heat the jelly and, if you like, add a bit of fruit brandy or liqueur.

1 (8-ounce) package nonfat cream cheese (bar type, not
   spreading type)
⅓ cup sugar
¼ cup nonfat sour cream
1 teaspoon vanilla extract
1 9-inch (6-ounce) prepared graham cracker crust
3 cups small or medium strawberries
⅓ cup red currant jelly
1 teaspoon kirsch or other fruit brandy (optional)

Cut cream cheese into a few pieces and let soften slightly. Beat in a mixing bowl until smooth. Beat in sugar, followed by sour cream and vanilla. Pour into crust. Refrigerate, uncovered, while preparing strawberries.

Rinse and hull strawberries. Pat dry. Halve them lengthwise. Arrange them on top of cream cheese filling, beginning at outer edge of pie and placing them cut side down.

Melt jelly with 2 teaspoons water in a small saucepan over low heat, stirring often. Off heat, stir in kirsch. Cool slightly. Brush or spoon jelly over berries; spoon any remaining jelly in spaces between them. Refrigerate uncovered about 30 minutes or until ready to serve. If there is any leftover pie, refrigerate it uncovered.

Makes 6 servings.

CHOCOLATE CINNAMON APPLESAUCE CAKE

Cocoa and cinnamon combine to give this easy-to-make cake a great flavor, while applesauce and a small amount of oil contribute a pleasing, light texture. When you taste this cake, you won't believe it's low in fat.

1½ cups all-purpose flour
⅓ cup unsweetened cocoa
1½ teaspoons ground cinnamon
1 teaspoon baking soda
3 tablespoons vegetable oil
1 cup sugar
1 large egg
1⅓ cups applesauce

Preheat oven to 350°F. Coat a 9-inch square baking pan with oil spray; flour pan. Sift flour with cocoa, cinnamon, and baking soda. In a large bowl, beat oil, sugar, and egg at medium speed until pale in color and fluffy. On low speed, stir flour mixture alternately with applesauce into egg mixture; mix well.

Bake in prepared pan for 25 to 30 minutes, or until a cake tester inserted in cake comes out clean. Turn out onto a rack or leave in the pan; cool completely. Serve at room temperature. *Cake can be kept, covered, 4 days.*

Makes 16 servings.

FRESH KIWI SAUCE

Cool, refreshing, and relatively low in calories, this soft green sauce is ready in minutes. It makes tasty desserts with sliced peaches, nectarines, or mango, or spooned around sliced angel food cake topped with raspberries. Kiwi sauce is also a good accompaniment for fruit sorbets.

1¼ pounds kiwi
¾ cup confectioners' sugar, or to taste

Peel kiwi and cut into quarters. Puree kiwi with sugar in food processor until smooth. Leave sauce unstrained if you like the texture of the seeds. For a smooth sauce, strain sauce without pressing on pulp. Taste, and add more sugar if needed. Refrigerate until ready to serve. *Sauce can be kept, covered, 2 days in refrigerator.*

Makes 4 or 5 servings.

CONVERSION CHART

LIQUID MEASURES				SOLID MEASURES				OVEN TEMPERATURE EQUIVALENTS			
				U.S. and Imperial Measures		Metric Measures					
Fluid Ounces	U.S. Measures	Imperial Measures	Milliliters	Ounces	Pounds	Grams	Kilos	Farenheit	Gas Mark	Celsius	Heat of Oven
	1 tsp.	1 tsp.	5	1		28		225	1/4	107	Very Cool
1/4	2 tsp.	1 dessert spoon	7	2		56		250	1/2	121	Very Cool
1/2	1 T.	1 T.	15								
1	2 T.	2 T.	28	3-1/2		100		275	1	135	Cool
2	1/4 cup	4 T.	56	4	1/4	112		300	2	148	Cool
4	1/2 cup or 1/4 pint		110	5		140		325	3	163	Moderate
		1/4 pint or 1 gill	140	6		168		350	4	177	Moderate
6	3/4 cup		170								
8	1 cup or 1/2 pint		225	8	1/2	225		375	5	190	Fairly Hot
9			250 (1/4 liter)	9		250	1/4	400	6	204	Fairly Hot
10	1-1/4 cups	1/2 pint	280	12	3/4	340		425	7	218	Hot
12	1-1/2 cups or 3/4 pint		340	16	1	450		450	8	232	Very Hot
15		3/4 pint	420	18		500	1/2	475	9	246	Very Hot
16	2 cups or 1 pint		450	20	1-1/4	560					
18	2-1/4 cups		500 (1/2 liter)	24	1-1/2	675					
20	2-1/2 cups	1 pint	560								
24	3 cups or 1-1/2 pints		675	27		750	3/4				
25		1-1/4 pints	700	28	1-3/4	780					
27	3-1/2 cups		750	32	2	900					
30	3-3/4 cups	1-1/2 pints	840								
32	4 cups or 2 pints or 1 quart		900	36	2-1/4	1000	1				
				40		1100					
35		1-3/4 pints	980								
36	4-1/2 cups		1000 (1 liter)	48	3	1350					
				54		1500	1-1/2				

INDEX

Red and Green Cole Slaw with Pink
   Grapefruit, 77–78
Red Cabbage Salad and Tangy Cucumber,
   132
Red Cabbage Salad with Apples, 123
Red kidney beans, in three-bean salad with
   herb dressing, 103–4
Red peppers. *See* Peppers
Red Salad, 112
Rice
   Basmati with vegetables and cilantro,
      52–53
   brown, with greens, 82
   brown, as substitute for bulgur wheat, 72
   brown, as substitute for quick barley, 111
   brown, tabbouleh, 138–39
   curried cabbage with, 65–66
   fat-free dish, 103
   jasmine, steamed, 93
   pilaf, 105
   Provençal with tricolor peppers, 44
   salad, with dried cranberries and
      walnuts, 144
   salad, with peas and peppers, 117
   salads, serving tips, 138
   vegetables added to, 64
   white, steamed long-grain, 90
   See also Grains
Rice milk, 11
Rice Noodle Salad with Peanut Dressing,
   131
Rice Salad with Dried Cranberries and
   Walnuts, 144
Rice Salad with Peas and Peppers, 117
Ricotta cheese, dessert tip for, 10
Roasted Pepper, Fresh Mozzarella, and
   Watercress Sandwich, 142–43
Roasted peppers. *See* peppers
Roasting, 13
Romaine lettuce
   and radish salad with oranges, 96
   as substitute for spinach, 25
   with three-bean salad, 102
   with toasted walnuts, 110
Rotini with Zucchini, Tomatoes, and Basil,
   26

Salad dressings. *See* Dressings, salad
Salad of Exotic Mushrooms, Baby Lettuce,
   and Toasted Pecans, 22
Salads, 129–48
   antipasto, 37
   baby lettuce and spinach with feta
      cheese, 88
   bean and beet, 30

black bean with red onions, tomatoes,
   and garlic-cumin dressing, 143
butter lettuce with mustard vinaigrette,
   45
carrot, cranberry, and water chestnut, 65
corn with peppers, French, 147
cucumber and red cabbage, 132
cucumber-pepper with walnut oil
   vinaigrette, 99–100
green, with water chestnuts and sesame
   dressing, 93
Israeli vegetable, 62
Mediterranean diced with capers, 35
mushrooms, baby lettuce, and toasted
   pecans, 22
ravioli, tomato, and lima bean, with
   pesto dressing, 146–47
red, peppers and plum tomatoes, 112
red cabbage with apples, 123
rice, with dried cranberries and walnuts,
   144
rice, with peas and peppers, 117
rice noodle with peanut dressing, 131
romaine and radish with oranges, 96
romaine with toasted walnuts, 110
spinach, with chickpeas and peppers, 26
three-bean with herb dressing, 103–4
tips, 42
tomato, with garlic and parsley, 69–70
tricolor, 135
zucchini with dill and green onions, 113
See also Dressings, salad; Slaws
Salad Supper with Chinese Flavors, A,
   129–32
Salsa
   avocado, 57
   as substitute for pepper dressing, 59
Sandwiches
   open-face, as appetizers, 142
   Soup and Sandwich, Italian Style menu,
      124–27
   Soup and Sandwich Lunch menu,
      107–10
Sauces, 15
   confetti vegetable, 38
   Hungarian pepper, 30–31
   mushroom-tomato, 151–52
   for pasta, 25
   sesame yogurt, 62
   sweet-and-sour, 83
   tomato, 15, 25, 104
   yogurt, 15, 73
Sauces, dessert
   blackberry, 27
   kiwi, 155
Sautéing, 13, 86

in rotini with zucchini and basil, 26–27
salad with garlic and parsley, 69–70
sauce, 15, 25, 104
in tortilla soup with green chiles, 116
zucchini and corn medley with, 74
Tortilla Soup with Green Chiles and
Tomatoes, 116
Tricolor Salad, 135
Tuscan Bean Soup with Pasta, 126

USDA Food Guide Pyramid, 2–4

Vanilla Ice Cream with Fresh Blackberry
Sauce, 27
Vegan menu tips, 20, 30, 36, 86
Vegetable broth, 32, 69, 95, 112
Vegetable Burrito Brunch, 54–57
Vegetable One-Pot Menus, 85–105
Vegetables, 4–5
Basmati rice and cilantro with, 52–53
in confetti sauce for linguine, 38
cooking techniques, 12–17
Israeli salad, 62
Moroccan stew, 96–97
puree as thickener, 108
ratatouille, 87
super-quick pizza, 122
See also Salads; specific vegetables
Vegetable Soup with Silver Noodles, Tofu,
and Cilantro, 91
Vegetarian Cassoulet, 100–101
Vegetarian Chili in a Hurry, 47–48
Vegetarian Paella, 70
Vinaigrette(s)
mustard, 45
preparing, 108
walnut oil, 99–100
Vinegar, 25

Walnut oil
fat and nutrient content, 108
vinaigrette, 99–100
Walnuts
in rice salad with dried cranberries, 144
toasted, with romaine salad, 110
Warm Weather Brunch, 137–40
Water chestnuts
in green salad with sesame dressing, 93
in salad with carrots and cranberries, 65

Yellow Squash in Sweet-and-Sour Sauce,
83
Yogurt
with beets and dill, 66
berries with, 36
frozen, as substitute for ice cream, 25, 27,
49
frozen, in chocolate orange coupe, 45
low or nonfat brand preferences, 10
in mango milkshake, 53
plain vs. flavored, 20
sauce, 15, 73
sauce, sesame, 62
spiced, carrots and corn with, 139
in strawberry-banana smoothie, 84
sweet potatoes with mint-accented,
75
as thickener in blender drinks, 81
vanilla, in strawberry-banana-orange
medley, 23

Zucchini
and corn medley with tomatoes, 74
in ratatouille, 87
in rotini with tomatoes and basil, 26–27
salad with dill and green onions, 113
as substitute for green beans, 130

ABOUT THE AUTHOR

Award-winning author Faye Levy is a "Grand Diplôme" graduate of the famed La Varenne Cooking School in Paris, where she studied and worked closely with the school's chefs for nearly six years. For the past seven years Faye has been a nationally syndicated cooking columnist for the *Los Angeles Times* Syndicate, focusing in her columns on quick, practical ways to cook delicious, low-fat meals. She has also written many articles for *Gourmet, Bon Appétit,* and other food magazines.

Faye has long had a keen interest in vegetarian cooking, and enjoys teaching cooking classes on vegetable dishes that are healthful and easy to prepare. *Faye Levy's International Vegetable Cookbook* won the James Beard Cookbook Award as the best book of 1994 in the category of Fruits, Vegetables and Grains. Levy also won cookbook awards from the International Association of Culinary Professionals for *Vegetable Creations* and for *Classic Cooking Techniques.* Her most recent cookbook is *30 Low-Fat Meals in 30 Minutes.*

Faye and her husband/associate, Yakir Levy, write, cook, and grow vegetables and fruit in Woodland Hills, California.